YIN YANG

YIN YANG

THE ELUSIVE SYMBOL THAT EXPLAINS THE WORLD

BY JACK RASMUSSEN

MANUSCRIPTS
PRESS

YIN YANG

The Elusive Symbol That Explains the World

ISBN

979-8-88926-752-2 *Paperback*

979-8-88926-518-4 *Hardcover*

979-8-88926-753-9 *Ebook*

Table of Contents

"Another well-conceived contribution to the mindfulness literature. Jack Rasmussen's book *Yin Yang* reminds us that [the practice of] mindfulness offers [us] a fulcrum for achieving a balance between the active and passive, constructive and letting go (flow) aspects of our daily existence."

—EDMUND J. BOURNE, PH.D., AUTHOR OF

THE ANXIETY & PHOBIA WORKBOOK

"'If you have a little spiritual knowledge, you should share it. This is the best type of charity.' This [sentiment] is a teaching from my guru. In sharing these teachings, Jack Rasmussen is helping to dispel a little of the darkness of ignorance."

—SRI DHARMA MITTRA, FOUNDER AND

DIRECTOR OF DHARMA YOGA CENTER

"I found *Yin Yang* to be a truly fascinating book. I read it at a time when I, like so many others, was experiencing burnout. This book is the perfect antidote to the problem. I especially enjoyed learning about Jack's own very personal experiences. I was particularly moved and inspired by his vulnerability in sharing past struggles. I would thoroughly recommend *Yin Yang*. It is a book that everyone needs to read in this extremely chaotic and complex modern world in which we all live today."

—JONNY BENJAMIN, AUTHOR, FILMMAKER, AND FOUNDER

OF YOUTH MENTAL HEALTH CHARITY BEYOND

"Few authors can tackle such a profound concept with sophistication and versatility. Rasmussen has done both. Great read!"

"*Yin Yang: The Elusive Symbol That Explains the World* by Jack Rasmussen is an enlightening exploration of balance and consciousness. Rasmussen's dedication to comprehending the yin-yang symbol, inspired by his experiences in Taiwan, reveals the profound interplay between light and dark, action and rest, and spirituality and mindfulness. His vibrant storytelling transports readers to the dynamic streets of Taipei, reflecting the essence of yin and yang. What distinguishes this book is Rasmussen's emphasis on mindfulness, a potent tool in today's stress-laden world. His conversations with spiritual leaders such as Sadhguru and Bawa Jain enrich his quest for self-awareness and happiness. This book is essential reading for those in search of a more purposeful life. Rasmussen's ability to unite spirituality, mindfulness, and practical wisdom makes "Yin Yang" indispensable for leaders, coaches, scholars, and anyone embarking on the journey to a balanced and gratifying life. It serves as a reminder that balance is not merely a destination but an ongoing voyage, with Rasmussen's insights illuminating the path ahead."

"In an age where educators and school leaders are consumed with the superficial task of scoring better on standardized tests, *Yin Ying* is a breath of fresh air. True education is the liberation of the mind, body, and soul, and this book provides an insightful blueprint for achieving true personal success. I would highly recommend this book to any educator who considers themselves to be more than test prep coordinators."

—ANTHONY MUHAMMAD, AUTHOR OF
OVERCOMING THE ACHIEVEMENT GAP TRAP

"Jack Rasmussen recounts his own discovery of the ancient concept of yin and yang, and he opens the way to a vast philosophy. His personal story is supported by thorough research, and he asks us to consider the most crucial personal and social issues of our times. *Yin Yang: The Elusive Symbol That Explains the World* fulfills an exciting journey. Along the way, we can discover yin and yang in our own lives."

—DENG MING-DAO, AUTHOR OF *365 TAO, THE LUNAR TAO, SCHOLAR WARRIOR,* AND *CHRONICLES OF TAO*

"In *Yin Yang*, Jack Rasmussen helps us unravel how to navigate our chaotic lives. His writing about complex ideas is relatable. This book will help us move forward into a better future. *Yin Yang* is about duality, balance, and

understanding how to live a centered life. It's an enticing and accessible look at how we can live our best lives."
—SEAN PRENTISS, AUTHOR OF *FINDING ABBEY: THE SEARCH FOR EDWARD ABBEY AND HIS HIDDEN DESERT GRAVE*

"In *Yin Yang: The Elusive Symbol That Explains the World*, Jack leaves no stone unturned as he shares his understanding of the various ways in which the dual nature of life presents itself in our world. As one who grew up in the West and then traveled to the East to immerse himself in a culture with a rich history of contemplation, Jack offers diverse perspectives and philosophies in which we can each find a source of knowledge that resonates with us deeply and across many areas. Covering topics such as mindset, leadership, relationships, entertainment, and business, he makes a compelling case for a deeper understanding of how we are best served by intentionally engaging with life while transparently sharing his own stories. What I love about Jack's book is his exploration of the cyclical nature of life, first inspired by the Yin Yang and all that it symbolizes about duality, balance, and ebb and flow. I had a moment of clarity when the dots connected; the Yin Yang is the perfect representation of my lifelong fascination with its themes."
—MAKI MOUSSAVI, AUTHOR OF *THE HIGH ACHIEVER'S GUIDE*

"*Yin Yang: The Elusive Symbol That Explains the World*
by Jack Rasmussen is an outstanding book meant to help
the reader make sense of the world and understand that
balance is a gift you can give yourself once you allow space
for it to thrive in your life. Exhaustion, anger, and anxiety
will diminish as you balance your time and consciously set
out to become more grounded and live with a meditative
state of mind. Using his skilled art of storytelling to cap-
tivate the reader, Rasmussen is willing to be vulnerable in
order to teach lessons of mindfulness and convey effective
ways to find peace in today's fast-paced world. Embrace
the author's sound advice and use it to understand how to
bring Yin Yang into your daily life."

—BRUCE LANGFORD, MINDFULNESS MODE
PODCAST CREATOR AND HOST

"The world has been chaotic and will still be so for many
years. But from the perspective of a Taoist philosopher,
everything is nothing but yin and yang. The formula of
happiness or good resolution for everything is yin yang
balance. Rasmussen, with his book, all the more strengthens such a point!"

—MASTER GU SHINING, FOUNDER OF THE
WUDANG TAOIST WELLNESS ACADEMY

"Jack tackles complexity with beauty and relatability, uncovering how duality can shape greatness in us all."
—HILARY DECESARE, INTERNATIONAL BUSINESS COACH, TRANSFORMATIONAL EXPERT, AND CEO OF THE RELAUNCH CO.

"I admire Jack's drive for self-improvement."
—BRIAN BRUYA, EDITOR OF *EFFORTLESS ATTENTION* (MIT PRESS)

In memory of Pops.

I dedicate this book to the gorgeous country of Taiwan (my home for a year) and my serene hosts on my journey: Green World Hotel Taipei Station, Fullon Hotel Tamsui Fisherman's Wharf, Éclat Hotel Taipei, Great Skyview Hotel, Dazhi Denwell, Green World Hotel Zhonghua, Kindness Hotel Zhongshan Bade, The Great Roots Forestry Spa Resort, W Taipei, Four Points by Sheraton Penghu, Discovery Hotel, Pescadores Resort, Tai Hu Hotel Sun Moon Lake, Cloudenjoy B&B, Caesar Metro Hotel Taipei, Shangri-La Far Eastern Tainan, Qi Shiseido Salon and Spa, Longshan Temple, Chimei Museum, National Museum of Taiwan Literature, and The Museum of World Religions. The visits were magical.

Foreword

When we face problems, we try to find ways to tackle them. In Buddhism one of our pertinent teachings is the avoidance of extremes. Similarly, nurturing compassion for others while maintaining a positive and comprehensive outlook on life is something that can help in one's inner development.

When faced with difficulties, we should look at the problem from multiple dimensions and not from one angle alone. In this book, Jack Rasmussen shares his personal experience and explores ways to look at life positively. I hope readers find it helpful.

2 November 2023

Prologue

I was hungover. Bad. I walked into the church, nauseated and chaotic. I did not know if my friends knew it, and I did not care. But I did feel bad.

Church, which for me is a modern, large building in Glendale, is my happy place. It gives me a sense of relief, hope, and community in my often-noisy life.

I had gone to The Bungalow in Santa Monica the night before. The Bungalow was a restaurant my friends and I frequented— plush with a pool table, ping pong table, and several indoor and outdoor bars. Cocaine and a Moscow mule was my signature combination. It was always euphoric but short-lived. I listened to the preacher, my good friend, to accept God's grace. *Oh boy*, I thought, *I need that bad.*

I prayed a lot that day because I knew my social life was driving me to do crazy things that I had to tell God to forgive me for consistently. I would make excuses in my head like *I am only young once*, or, *This will not happen once I graduate.*

The problem was alcohol allowed me to escape my loneliness and the pressure I felt. Naturally, I am a workaholic. I do not know when to stop. I find it hard to relax. I always have.

Taking communion and returning to my seat to listen to the final song from the band, I chewed on the bread and washed it down with grape juice like an animal that had not eaten in days. I probably hadn't. I waved goodbye to my friends and returned to my South Central, Los Angeles house, feeling refreshed for my busy academic week ahead.

One of the most exciting parts of my week was my class called Asian Aesthetic and Literary Traditions. Being the only white man in my discussion class of twenty Asian students was interesting, and I loved it. We covered the *Tao Te Ching* and several Buddhist texts. I learned more about Daoism, Buddhism, and Confucianism—three Asian religions I have always been intrigued by because of their highly philosophical feeling.

It was a moment in my highly energetic, often drug-induced, free-flowing week to explore religious scripture and the meaning of life—two things that have captured my attention since I was young because of my natural curiosity. I find myself gazing at poetry by Matsuo Basho, drawn to his imagery and delicate portrait of nature to mirror humanity and its beauty. I read "The Old Pond" multiple times, a haiku about a frog leaping into a pond. Simple, so it seemed.

I raised my hand.

"The frog represents interruption. No matter how long one can stay at peace, there will always be an interruption in the silence or the current moment," I offered. "Nothing lasts forever, no matter how hard you may try."

The teacher looked at me and responded, "Yes. That is impermanence."

I was intrigued by impermanence because it offers hope. Every day is a new day. One day, I woke up dizzy. The next day, I woke up feeling extremely clear. One day, I received a threat. The next day, someone bought me lunch.

I wanted to dive deeper into impermanence, nonattachment, and this cyclical nature of life. I understood that both ideas of impermanence and humanity's connected, formless spirit were central themes in Daoism and Buddhism. Much like some of my Christian learning, when we reject ourselves and our physical manifestation, we connect deeper with others and are naturally happier.

In my short twenty-two years of life, I have broken many hearts, made many enemies, and met several people I call friends. But life goes on. What intrigues me is my introduction to religion, and specifically, East Asian religion, opened up a new perspective on my compulsive life of destruction. I began to meditate. I began to embrace this idea of being formless, presented by Lao Tzu, Taoist master, in the *Tao Te Ching*.

I craved more. I went to Sunset Boulevard in Los Angeles and bought a new hat. The hat had a symbol on it, a sign that would come to represent the next year of my life. That symbol is called yin yang and represents balance, fusion, and surrender to me.

And my pursuit of letting go to trust the universe's purpose for me began.

I decided to leave for Asia for a year.

PART 1:

DEEP HISTORY

Introduction to Taiwan

"A good heart, Kate, is the sun and the moon—or rather the sun and not the moon, for it shines bright and never changes, but keeps his course truly. If thou would have such a one, take me: and take me, take a soldier: take a soldier, take a king."

—WILLIAM SHAKESPEARE, HENRY V, ACT 5 SCENE 2

We all need balance to reach a sense of personal peace.

The yin-yang symbol (also called the tai chi symbol) is a beautiful representation of this fruitful state of balance. The English Chi (Ji in pinyin) 极 (meaning extreme) is different from the Chi (Qi in pinyin) 氣 (meaning gas, air). Qi is understood as an energy force that powerfully flows through the body. The act of tai chi is said to promote the flow of qi. Yin and yang represent opposing elements that make up the universe and must be kept in harmony. Tai chi helps foster this balance. In this book, I will refer to tai chi as creating or influencing chi, qi, or life force energy within the body. The chi in tai chi directly means chi or ji. Tai chi translates to "supreme ultimate" and deals with life force energy or qi. This "chi" represents the energy that flows through our body and unites us and the rest of the world.

When I arrived in Taipei, Taiwan, in early August of 2022 for my Fulbright scholarship awarded to me by US Congress, I was dizzy and exhausted. I stepped off the airplane onto a runway at Taiwan Taoyuan International Airport as the summer humidity hit me hard, blanketing me in moisture. The buildings off into the distance were tall, gray, and close together. The skyline reminded me of San Francisco—vast, populated mountains sitting green and neat behind the buildings, one more elevated than the others (Taipei 101).

I went through customs, received a new phone and phone number, and a guard led me through what felt like an obstacle course to finally reach my cab to take me to my hotel in downtown Taipei. The scenery of Taipei was beautiful as I peered out my window: lush and green landscapes, buildings of all different colors, roads intersecting like a game of Twister, and pedestrians everywhere.

Pedestrians were biking and walking—none without a mask covering their face and clothes covering their bodies. Scooters were almost as present as cars, weaving in and out of traffic like gazelles. The city was full of vibrant city-scape noise. Primary color temples, lots of 7-Elevens and Family Marts, old high-rises, and modern skyscrapers fill the downtown area. The area around each temple featured the natural beauty of aesthetic parks filled with green vegetation and decorative stone statues. The air smelled of fresh Pacific Ocean, fried food, and smoke.

I could hear cars honking, scooters accelerating, people eating, and mutters of Mandarin that I could barely make out. I saw Mandarin characters everywhere I looked—on buildings, cars, and street signs. I had entered a foreign context where I felt a newfound sense of adventure and the desire to discover.

I reached my hotel, a modern green and gold building on a busy street filled with nonstop-moving scooters and cars. I felt excited and nervous as I entered the hotel, signed my name, and began a five-day quarantine period.

I slowly acclimated as I peered out of my Green World Hotel window into the buzzing and magnificent view of downtown Taipei at 5 a.m.: eager scooter riders, pedestrians excitedly walking about in and out of the many street shops below, and the city skyline lighting up with the warm sunrise. Being from a small town in California and attending university in the south part of Los Angeles, I was not used to this amount of energy so early in the morning. I fell in love with the plethora of fun opportunities—from restaurants, temples, and museums to night markets, bubble tea, and friendly locals.

It was a beautiful and magical time for me. After meeting many Fulbright and Taiwanese government officials, I knew I had to write this book.

Religion has always been a massive part of my life.

I have always craved balance, and the Asian symbol of yin yang is of great importance to centeredness, collectiveness, and consciousness in Daoism/Taoism.

As a perpetual learner and traveler, digging deeper into a religious symbol and exploring my relationship with the sign in my life seemed extremely fun and essential for my growth in Asia.

I am a practicing Christian who attends church every weekend, reads the Bible, and prays regularly. The exploration of Daoism, Taoism, and Chinese Folk Religion (a combo of Confucianism, Taoism, and Buddhism) was an activity I wanted to do very much. I am very energetic, often with a monkey mind, and meditation has completely transformed my life and well-being.

This beautiful dichotomy (represented by yin and yang) in the human brain, lifestyle, and the world allows us to be the best versions of ourselves.

Awareness is the door to liberation, which everyone can unlock by reaching a higher level of consciousness through mindfulness.

How would it be if we lived life balanced, without always uncomfortably searching for the next bar to reach? Calm. Poised.

We often only think through some of the actions we take. We do them automatically and naturally. Without attachment, judgment, expectations, and assumptions, peace (both personal and worldly) would be so much easier to achieve. This society would be considered mindful. I mean aware, focused, present, engaged—not lost in the past or obsessed with the future.

A pure-hearted person, within the world of now eight billion people and counting, glued to the present moment as tightly as the moment flees from existence. One who truly realizes that the only time is now as the future does not exist and neither does the past.

The first step to this balance is being mindful. Mindfulness affects people positively; if more realize this, our world would be better. It is no secret that stress affects the body mentally and physically. To remove stress, we must eliminate our trauma by healing our past emotions and making ourselves aware of them to move on.

Mindfulness and contemplative sciences have been a growing field recently as our society, unfortunately, becomes more washed away by technological distractions and collective trends. People spend more time on their phones than in real life, bogged down by the compulsive need to respond and serve others rather than enjoy what is right in front of them: a beautiful life full of mystery, wonder, and awe.

STAYING CURIOUS AND FORGIVING: UNDERSTANDING WE CREATE THE STRESS IN OUR LIVES

Part of reaching balance in life is working with curiosity and awe while resting with curiosity and wonder. We can aid ourselves through contemplative sciences by taking long intentional breaks from technology to actively engage with the people and places around us, constantly willing to learn with an open mind and heart. When chatting with TEDx Speaker David Vago, fresh off his excursion with the fourteenth Dalai Lama, I uncovered contemplative sciences as a necessary rise in our world with the importance of meditation for any environment of life, whether wisdom-based or spiritually based.

Sadhguru, a yogi, mystic, and author of *Inner Engineering: A Yogi's Guide to Joy*, exclaims in his 2021 chat with Matthew McConaughey:

> "Your life is the way you experience it. It is not what is around you, but how you experience it" (Sadhguru 2021).

Life is what we make of it. It can be nothing, or it can be everything.

I often find solace and meaning when remembering the Biblical history of God creating the world. I also remember that everything after that creation was a product of humanity. I recognize that often people envision what they desire and go about creating that vision without any sense of gratitude or self-awareness. My religion helps inform my steps. Everyone needs a guiding light, whether religious or nonreligious, to aid them in their steps.

Being alive enables my happiness because I could be dead or, much worse, living and unable to be free. This concept has allowed my meditative friends and me to let go and be truly free, welcoming the waves into our lives and riding them without force. I often think of a concept I learned about in Asia called "Wu Wei," which means without force. Rather than acting compulsively, to be content, we must act consciously—like sailing in the Taiwan Strait.

An often-common problem today is that some folks are unhappy or not living a life that is authentic to them. This problem may be due to forcing what is wrong or fighting with what the universe has planned for you.

Doctor Gabor Maté, one of the leading experts on the connection between the mind-body and illness, proclaims in "Dr. Gabor Maté on the Connection between Stress and Disease" that the most significant stress in our lives is trying to be someone other than yourself (2019).

I ask many friends about their happiness; many do not know how to respond. The fact that this is not an innate understanding for them displays that happiness is not a priority in our lives, or people need to be mindful enough to understand what exactly makes them happy.

This lack of clarity may be because we cannot center ourselves and know what we want from life. Several of us, unfortunately, live compulsively rather than consciously, pushing through the day on a strict self-focused schedule without thinking of what could be between the hectic moments of high stress and high cortisol levels.

According to a 2021 UnivDatos Market Insights study on the Mindfulness Meditation Apps Market, in 2020, 79 percent of working adults suffered from work-related stress, which was 20 percent higher than 59 percent in 2018. According to a 2017 Harris Poll spotlighted by UnivDatos, 80 percent of working people in the United States were stressed due to their jobs, while the same percentage was affected by that stress. One must understand the meaning of balance to come to a point of balance (UnivDatos Market Insights 2021).

Essentially, God's will helps us truly let go. In this book, I will show you what I've learned about balance in these areas and, hopefully, ways to achieve health, happiness, and compassion.

YIN YANG: THE ULTIMATE BALANCE

The symbol epitomizes the human ability to balance itself as the light and darkness balance out a mountain impacted by a rising and setting sun. If every human could take advantage of the opposites in their lives, especially rest and action, they could harness their abilities to their fullest potential. When digging deeper into these numbers, it is clear that an epidemic of stress within the United States undoubtedly bleeds into depression and anxiety.

Mindfulness, spirituality, and balance can help reverse this problem of living as someone else due to pressure or anxiety.

In my interview with Bawa Jain, the brilliant founder of The Centre for Responsible Leadership, we shared about living within every single moment and our connection to spiritual guidance as being prominent in our lives.

Jain exclaimed, "The principle of spirituality is mind, body, and soul awareness."

I concur with his statement and believe that when we reflect on our being while connecting to a greater purpose, we know who we are and why we do what we do. The point is to organize the unorganized mind, clear the cluttered brain, and manifest a life that you truly want through intentionality and connectivity.

Throughout my teenage years, before turning twenty-two, I explored meditation applications such as Calm and Headspace to calm my mind and enter a more peaceful state when trying to sleep. I also began practicing simple yoga techniques after workouts or after meditations or prayers outside on the grass. This attachment to God and dedication to becoming intentional with my life and my purpose allows me to write this book from a pure perspective, wanting to discover and learn more about why balance is crucial in today's world.

According to my friend David Vago's 2017 TEDx Talk, "Self-Transformation through Mindfulness," given in Nashville, since 2000, there have been four thousand studies on mindfulness. The more one meditates, the more one gets from their frontoparietal control network, which directly supports meta-awareness (Vago 2017).

Mindfulness is becoming a prominent practice or trait in the world, meaning people desire to learn more about it, a necessary step to becoming more mindful. This intention is essential because mindfulness allows for the individual curation of a more purposeful and fulfilling life. Living clearly by simply being the best version of yourself without getting distracted by others' lives is crucial to living in peace. This goal is like balancing life as a sponge and stone (yin and yang), being both a perpetual learner and a go-getter and not needing validation to live authentically.

FINDING YOUR INNER YIN-YANG BALANCE: CRITICAL FOR ALL LEADERS AND COACHES

Individuals seeking a more balanced and fulfilling life who are spiritually mindful will love this book. This group includes religious leaders, mind-set coaches, meditation fanatics, anyone looking to become more spiritual or intentional with their actions, current and former Fulbright scholars, and academics or entrepreneurs who want to make meaningful changes in their societies.

During his April 2011 speech for The Tucker Foundation and Dartmouth Hitchcock Medical Center, Doctor Jon Kabat-Zinn discusses the fear of dying as paradoxically the fear of living. Essentially, we are consistently afraid to hit that finish line without fully embracing what is available now. Living wholly within the present moment defines mindfulness. Purposeful meditation and connected spirituality reduce unnecessary stress that blocks this dynamic presence (Kabat-Zinn 2011).

Yin Yang: The Elusive Symbol That Explains the World is critical to read because achieving balance through embracing your yin and yang is one of the essential qualities to be a successful human being in life. Spirituality helps us connect to ourselves and gain deeper self-awareness and awareness of others through inspiring deep mindfulness. Achieving balance isn't easy, or we would live in a peaceful world. It's important to remember to forgive our mistakes, to forgive others, and to do our best to grow toward a more harmonious way of being. I hope this book will point you toward what it means to live a fun, relaxed, and intention-filled life.

Weightlessness should not be a game of luck. Rather, weightlessness should be natural. I hope you will realize while reading this book that you are a human being, and your existence is enough to represent who you are. What you do is secondary. Get comfortable with doing nothing. Enjoy with a cup of overflowing joy.

Happy meditating!

CHAPTER 2

Introduction to Yin and Yang: Darkness and Daylight

THE WAVY BLACK AND WHITE SYMBOL

"Words and pictures are yin and yang. Married, they produce a progeny more interesting than either parent."
—DR. SEUSS

Duality. Two sides. Two contrasts. Two poles. The Earth has it. Our twenty-four hours has it. We, as human beings, need it as well. An ancient Chinese philosophical concept represents this spirit well; yin and yang embody this duality.

The yin-yang symbol, also known as the tai chi symbol, is a circle separated by a curved line with a black and white side, each with a small dot of the other color. Within yin, there is always yang, and within yang, there is yin.

Between my eighth- and seventh-grade English classes that I teach, I came across a February 16, 2021 episode entitled "The Duality of Yin & Yang" by the Spotify podcast *Yin: Untangled—Yin Yoga with Cat Mead*.

She explains that yin is darker, passive, and restful while yang is hot, active, light, doing, and energetic. As earthlings, we must be able to see the opposing view as we cannot have one without the other. Meaning we need one to measure whether the opposite exists. For example, we can only say something is cold by knowing when it is hot. Therefore, according to this wavy symbol, we live paradoxically. There are no absolute terms, and the states are fluid. We switch between these two different—opposite—energies all the time (Mead 2021).

Growing up, I was always intrigued by the sun and the moon. I became even more intrigued in first grade once I learned that the sun reflects upon the moon because I realized they have a strong relationship beyond being in space together. The moon needs the sun for the light within our very black night sky, and the sun embraces the moon as a blocking mechanism to allow Earthlings to get a break from its at-times overwhelming heat. This dynamic captivated me. I went home to ask my parents, grandparents, and friends questions.

I became obsessed with this idea of opposites or pairs. I asked: "Why does everything have an opposite?" I also asked: "Does everyone have one specific soul mate in the world that is perfect for them? How do you know what goes with what? Who decides what goes with what? How do we figure this out?"

In my ten-year-old mind, I was filing: peanut butter and jelly, Tom and Jerry, Phineas and Ferb, Scooby-Doo and Shaggy, burger and fries, and ketchup and mustard. I was thinking about what made the world combine these two things. Then I thought they each must bring something to the table that the other does not have. One is sweet, and the other is savory; one is protein-packed, and the other is starchy; one is loud, and the other is quiet; one is fast, and the other is slow; one is forward-thinking, and the other is reflective. I was starting to understand that in life, there are undeniable complements. I looked at my mom and dad and understood that one was female and the other was male.

Fast-forward twelve years, and I am sitting in an office building diving into an Asian symbol that has since captured my attention by explaining the art of duality deeper and further. Yin yang represents forces that are opposite but interconnected. I think back to my curious mind wondering about the sun and the moon, the male and the female, and brightness and darkness. I smile because this white and black symbol unpacks a full-circle moment of curiosity, discovery, and enlightenment. However, as a twenty-two-year-old, I recognize that the lines of division and intersection are not always black and white.

Mead thinks we should free ourselves from the thought that yang is solely masculine and yin is exclusively feminine. Indeed, femininity is sometimes viewed as weak. It is no secret that men often think they must be masculine, and females grow up adhering to the fact that they must be feminine and pretty to be attractive to men. Categories are toxic and unnecessary, but society pressures us to be one or the other.

Before we begin this journey together, it is crucial to separate yin and yang from the sex of humans because we need both aspects in ourselves. Each element explored in the book is conceptual and explains why having this duality within us or a particular life situation is warranted and highly necessary to succeed.

Yin and yang act as a lens for the book as it stands for dichotomy or a fine line and a physical manifestation symbolizing that seeing and being both sides is critical for success. Picture energy as two sides of the mountain. The sunny side is the yang, and the shady side is the yin. The hill is balanced by feeling both of these sides. This balance is analogous to the human—needing to feel the sun and the shade, needing to feel the spotlight, and needing solitude.

THE OFTEN-*GLORIFIED* YANG AND THE EQUALLY NECESSARY YIN
It is no secret that society glorifies yang—getting things done and staying continuously busy. However, we need to feel the opposing energy to feel the current energy productively. In other words, understanding the contrasting emotion of our present emotions is essential to enjoy and be aware of our feelings.

Yin represents the inner soul. When using the term "inner soul," I mean the feelings inside of us, allowing us to expose our deepest emotions. Mead explains that both yin and yang have meridian lines. First, yin has the heart (the act of "just being"), and yang has the small intestine or the act of "filling and emptying." Yin has a hidden line of energy (darker), and yang has a line of power outside the body (lighter). This fact explains why yin yoga targets our darker sides, focusing on passive tissues while moving slowly (joints, ligaments, bones).

Yang parts are the muscles that are used during an action. Psychologist Carl Jung stated: "Human beings live in a continuous contraction." Jung meant that we continuously search for balance between our two sides, whether we like it or not. The yin and yang would be connected to both contraction and expansion, which are both never-ending within a cycle we deem life. The sensations of contraction and expansion within the body create this duality continuously inside the body as we breathe, move, and live (Mead 2021).

Another way to understand contraction and expansion is to understand further tai chi postures, an exercise born out of the practice of Taoism and the concept of yin and yang. Once a person practices tai chi a lot, they will understand all movements come from their torso. Postures such as "High Pat on Horse" and "Brush Knee Twist Step" express the body movement expanding and contracting simultaneously. For example, in the "Brush Knee Twist Step," one hand pushes forward while the other pushes back on the thigh as the twist step is performed—out and in. Like the tai chi movement, humans juggle expression and reception concurrently daily.

According to Einzelgänger's 2019 video entitled "The Deep Meaning of Yin & Yang," "being" is considered to be yang, while "nonbeing" is considered yin. Nothing can exist without both, and defining the halves within something depends on the relationship between the two. While yin is often overlooked, it contains a lot of expressive power. One of the most critical aspects of yin is emptiness. A mug, for example, is a handy tool representing yin because it holds space for coffee or tea to enter. Our solar system would not exist if there were not any space to store the planets in our solar system. Yin also represents rest and passivity. Despite being heavily looked down upon, taking breaks and slowing down is essential. The video rightfully announces:

"Passivity is essential for every form of accomplishment" (Einzelgänger 2019).

For instance, muscles grow at rest, and our memory strengthens from quality sleep. A critical piece of yin is receptiveness, and this receptiveness couples brilliantly with any yang coupling. A yin and yang team and the yin and yang dynamic within us continue to recycle because when one becomes too dominant, the other side grows until it becomes too prevalent. This overtaking is a continuous cycle within us.

Lao Tzu, the creator of Daoism, wrote about this paradoxical dynamism that is essential for the world to move forward. He noted that movement is only possible if a countermovement has been made before.

Within chapter 36 of the *Tao Te Ching*, Lau Tzu wrote:

"If you want something to return to the source,
you must first allow it to spread out.
If you want something to weaken,
you must first allow it to become strong.
If you want something to be removed,
you must first allow it to flourish.
If you want to possess something,
you must first give it away" (Laozi 1995).

The dance of both feminine and masculine is ever-changing, complementary, and flowing at all times. Perhaps the key is knowing when you should enforce more yin or yang—whether to back off or get involved or whether being enthusiastic or clingy will have destructive consequences.

A film premiered at the 2022 Venice Film Festival called *Don't Worry Darling* (2022) explains this yin and yang dichotomy well. I enjoyed watching the movie with Mandarin subtitles at the new state-of-the-art Pier 3 Mall in Magong Harbor. At the Venice Film Festival press conference featuring Olivia Wilde, Harry Styles, Gemma Chan, and Chris Pine, Director Olivia Wilde explains Pine's character, the story's main antagonist: "That's one of the main tenets of Frank's philosophy is that chaos is destructive, and that control leads to beauty and perfection" (Titanium Magazine 2022).

The psychological thriller aims to illustrate that controlling people never leads to utopia, as it is simply not human nature. If one attempts to tame nature (as Frank does in this fictitious society in the film called "Victory"), they directly oppose Mother Nature. This forced contraction demonstrates the need for a natural push and pull in life—the contracted and expanded aspects of emotions and sensations. Controlling these unforced sensations, our genuine feelings, bodies, or mother nature can lead to destruction or further chaos. In other words, the disorder is organic and forced control is never a good idea. A theme deliberately arises—chaos versus structure (Wilde 2022).

Humans naturally attempt to control what is before us—a consistently changing and chaotic environment. Instead, rest (yin) comes without force. Control is a human creation that should never be attempted to attain. The whole purpose of yin and yang is to surrender to life's waves and cycles and plan for you rather than egotistically forcing your plan. Self-love can help us let go of our ego and enjoy naturally flowing between expansion and contraction without drugs, rigid structure, or judgment.

> One of the great forces that balances our two poles is meditation, self-love, and compassion for others and the world.

I remember when I first arrived in Taipei. The scene was chaotic because I was meeting so many people for the first time, and there were so many scooters on the street rushing to get to places. I was twenty-one, which meant I could do almost anything: drink, drive, enter clubs, and hang out with all different kinds of locals. Because I could not speak the language well and I was in an entirely new environment, I had a sense of freedom that I had never had before. It was overwhelming, and I ended up sleeping a lot. I slept a lot, not only because I was jet lagged but because it gave me some sense of control amidst the chaos. I needed a lot of rest or yin to balance out the activity of taking action (yang) into the unknown.

I also turned to religion, reading my Bible from home and getting lost in the temples of Taiwan to calm down and pray. When I arrived on the Penghu Islands from the mainland of Taiwan at the beginning of August, one of the first things I noticed was the number of temples in the county. In August, I had the pleasure of visiting them after researching the Tzu Chi Foundation. I had the pleasure of meeting and conversing with the workers in the building, devoted to their craft. According to the Tzu Chi organization website, the Tzu Chi Foundation was created by Venerable Dharma Master Cheng Yen on the poor east coast of Taiwan.

I love the principle that endlessly guides her innovative creation: "Help the poor and educate the rich" (Tzu Chi Foundation 2014).

Yen feels that the lack of selfless love for others is the cause of many problems in this world. She recognized that material poverty was not the sole contributor to the world's downfall but spiritual poverty, especially among the rich. The incredible organization, founded on the principles of Buddhism teaching, serves to help those in need through volunteering efforts. Cheng, now a famous religious leader in all of Asia and sometimes referred to as "Mother Teresa of Asia," had justly focused the foundation on medicine, education, environmental protection, international relief work, and creating a marrow donor registration.

Whether represented in media, religion, or the day-to-day working of human beings, the duality and dichotomy of human nature are abundantly present. They must be for these structures or current events to continue naturally. This book will explore the necessary duality of human nature through art, geography, and religion to examine why exploring the light and dark poles within yourself is essential to maintain a consistent, balanced, and compassionate life.

It was Thursday, December 1, in Penghu. The winds were tumultuous, and the rain was beginning to pick up. I had been texting back and forth with a brilliant spiritual leader named Nandhiji Adhipen Bose (also known as Nandhiji Tapasyogi for his yoga teaching), based in India. Bose is the chairman of CNESS Inc., the founder of World Yogi Day and Declaration of Consciousness, and the author of *Mastery of Consciousness*. Between a tour of my school for a college friend and lunch at a local beef noodle place by the regional airport, Bose sent me long responses to some questions I was curious about. Specifically, Nandhiji, who calls me "Divine Jack," as I believe he does all his friends, elaborated on this continual conversation about how we carried around the darkness and light inside and outside us.

In light our purest form of mindfulness and self-love can grow. Where exactly we think from determines the soundness and worthiness of each thought; within the layering of onion peeling of the conscious mind, beautiful wisdom can sprout. Specifically, Nandhiji's Buddhist faith explores the very core of the yin-yang symbol—spirituality's power in centering us. He says:

> Spirituality is liberation from limits of karma and karmic patterns and evolving nature of the animal to human to the divine. The balance in this journey of evolution is in aligning realities, i.e., translating our wisdom and knowing to action and Being. A vital dimension of progress in spirituality is grace that comes from aligning action—Dharma.

Nandhiji labels this connection to light as the "lamp." Once lit, the journey upward is never-ending, and troubles such as addiction and past trauma fall away naturally. As a guide, teacher, mentor, and Guru, Nandhiji has watched several students navigate the darkness and light within themselves and transform in healing ways.

As we discussed religion, we understood that within that umbrella lives faith, rituals, and fellowship between disciples, only made possible through reaching a higher self: liberated, mindful, and whole.

The yin-yang symbol promotes a balanced state of mind and, I believe, a form of being that is at peace. I like to call this living with and through your heart. Nandhiji calls this center inside us our "core." Being wide awake and hyperaware of this flowing state in our bodies that is inherently connected to the rest of the orbiting world is a step to discovering what we truly want and living authentically from within. Peace is so simple and easy when we live from within, like a beautiful love song. Nandhiji expanded on this enlivened "core" idea:

> When our core is awake, we know the bliss of Being that is joyful, inspired, vibrant and inner sun awake, happy. Peacefulness is our nature. Light our lamp within and awaken the core within that becomes each delicious eternal moment's journey. Experience all of life's ups and downs and the mind in its cyclical happiness and sadness knowing the core as our personal realm where we plunge within and arise a million times. Grow and evolve into the divine that is the sacred destiny within each of us.

Ultimately, yin yang (shadow/light), emotions/action, contraction/expansion, and control/chaos all lead to the importance of self-love and compassion. Anyone can unlock their higher self by understanding the balance of these complementary forces, and the power of living at peace with yourself and the world can illuminate unfettered. Stay lit. Stay burning. Stay aware.

TIME AND DEATH

I was in Taipei on Thursday, January 12, 2023, after finishing the Fulbright midyear conference at Great Roots Forestry

Spa Resort in Sanxia. I enjoyed visiting the Museum of World Religions in Yonghe District, New Taipei. Coincidentally, before my visit, the museum installed a beautiful new attraction called "Bright as Night, Dark as Day: A Walk with the Death."

I took my shoes off and looked left to read a quote by Zen Master Thich Nhat Hanh: "The meaning of life is hidden in every moment, every breath, and every step of the way."

The purpose of the exhibit is to confront death head-on. My interpretation was to rethink how we use our time to better utilize what we are given with a brand new, cleaner perspective to maximize life's seconds.

"Life is eternal, love is immortal, and death is only a horizon between dark and light"

—*KENNETH KRAMER, THE SACRED ART OF DYING*

If death is the in-between between dark night and daylight, perhaps it represents the line within the yin-yang symbol or the intersection of yin and yang. Maybe death drives the cycle in the first place—the fact that everything comes to an end.

The remarkable 2023 exhibition series explores the concept of "closure." The artwork on the wall ponders, "Is death a source of suffering in life, or a necessary factor for living a meaningful life?"

This remark is a great question that illuminates the purpose and importance of spirituality within our lives to understand ourselves while pondering our mortality and the afterlife. The beautiful exhibition provides an experiential adventure to inspire this essential consideration while enabling people to confront life's light and darkness bluntly and powerfully.

The wall features quotes from Heraclitus, Steve Jobs, Claude Lévi-Strauss, Master Hsin Tao, and Mahatma Gandhi—all leaders inspired by the concept of time and death. Accepting that all things come to an end pushes us to create, explore, and live in unknown territories.

> "Waking up means understanding life and how one should live it."
>
> —*MASTER HSIN TAO*

The exhibit following this quote by Master Hsin Tao was called "Internal Alarm." It was my favorite. Dark, gray concrete walls with papers taped haphazardly to the ceiling overlap. The documents had disturbing portraits or glaring questions that I do not often ask myself but believe I should more often:

1. Every life eventually comes to an end. So what do I want to accomplish the most at this moment?
2. If today was the last day of my life, what would I do?
3. To whom do I want to say "thank you," "sorry," and "I love you," respectively?

After drawing the yin-yang symbol on paper, relaxing in a landscape filled with white sand and roses, and walking through a tunnel of white feathers, I felt empowered and reminded myself that my past has happened, and I am where I am supposed to be. The only place for me to go is forward. The only time I have left is ahead of me. The only moment we have left is in front of us. How will we use it? You decide.

CHAPTER 3

Bones: Tai Chi and Mythology

"Don't let the behavior of others destroy your inner peace."
—*THE FOURTEENTH DALAI LAMA*

I woke up one morning in Taiwan, sluggish and worn out. I thought about the Taiwanese Zumba class I participated in over Zoom in August. I looked out my window and saw the crowded street in front of the daily market where I live, and I could already smell the fish being cut and prepared for the morning ahead and hear the hustle and bustle.

I sat back in bed and closed my eyes to pray and meditate.

In my head, I count. *One. Two. Three.*

I focus on my breath.

Sometimes, I use a guided meditation from my Calm or Headspace mobile application. Still, in Asia, I have mostly gravitated toward mindfulness meditations called samatha-vipassana, focusing on truth and healing while reflecting on my past trauma. The week prior, I did Zen meditation, focusing exclusively on living in the moment and nothingness.

Frequently, especially in Penghu, I will walk to the ocean and sit by the water to perform transcendental meditation in complete silence. As the waves ebb and flow, crashing on the sand, I replay a mantra: *Today will be a great day, Jack.*

Before or as I walk back home from the walkway along the shore, I try to perform walking meditations: tai chi, yoga, or qi gong. Tai chi is an activity that is very difficult to comprehend, and it is what you make of it. I laugh when I see older people in the park synchronized with funny movements involving their torso, back, and arms. Some so elegant and others so stiff. I gently move my hips and arms to connect my body with my soul. Although it may seem outlandish, it relaxes me.

Tai chi means the whole is greater than the assembled parts. The yin-yang symbol is a physical manifestation of this concept, bridging and interlocking two opposite worlds together, each globe making the other stronger like parallel, connected universes. The symbol has a piece of each color (black and white) within the different colors, a critical symbolism encompassing tai chi's theme of complete wholeness and stable balance. Tai chi helps to find mindfulness and reach a place of personal satisfaction by connecting to oneself and the universe.

According to Doctor Paul Lam, leader of the Tai Chi for Health Institute, tai chi is a self-run exercise that is an art form, exercising the health of mind and body. The action is practiced for health benefits and meditation, equating to extraordinary balance in one's life. Many people desire the achievement of balance, and tai chi is one fantastic avenue for attaining it. The connection between balance, yin yang, and tai chi is seamless, as the words are practically synonymous and interchangeable. The yin-yang symbol is the symbol for tai chi, and the purpose of the symbol is to represent a balance between complementary forces at play. These forces can be between people, within one person, or among the wider world. Performing tai chi allows one to connect to themselves while also connecting to the outside world, centering themselves in the present moment within the context of their own body and the outer galaxy at large (Lam 2022).

According to a May 16, 2018 article by Mark Cartwright in World History Encyclopedia, yin and yang are believed to have been created while the universe was being made, existing harmoniously at the center of the Earth (Cartwright 2018).

During the creation, the incredible achievement of balance allowed for the birth of Pangu (the first human). Ironically, the Taiwanese island I am writing this book on is called Penghu, oddly similar to the name of the first human, according to Chinese mythology. Also, due to this impeccable balance, the first gods named Fuxi, Nüwa, and Shennong were born (Cartwright 2018).

Interestingly enough, Taiwan has the highest density of religious buildings in Asia. As an American coming to an East Asian country for the first time, I was interested in individualism versus collectivism. In big cities, especially in the United States, individualism is much stressed over collectivism. According to the Internet Encyclopedia of Philosophy, "individualism" in the Asian context and culture does not represent autonomy and separation from authorities of power. Instead, individualism in Eastern thought denotes one's empowerment while feeling more unified with the country or outside authorities of power.

Whereas Western tradition often places individualism as a stratosphere of uniqueness and even isolationism, the Eastern tradition views individualism as a fabric of the larger connected socio-political realm of existence. In this way, "individualism" in Asian countries possesses a denotation a lot closer to what Americans understand as "collectivism." Scholars of early Chinese thought (Chad Hansen, Henry Rosemont, and Michael Nylan) consider "individualism" out of place in any Asian cultural study context. Most people view life in Asia as an "obligation and duty" without loads of freedom to explore individual pursuits (Brindley 2023).

According to the same IEP study, Confucianism emphasizes "self-cultivation" or "The Ru." In the *The Analects*, Confucius's important book, the *junzi* represents the highest ideal for an individual, only achieved through personal hard work involving training with the rites of the *Zhou* and in-depth moral education. So while individualism is not necessarily pushed for in Eastern contexts, Confucianism values self-cultivation, which alludes to some itch for self-involvement.

In addition, *Zhuangzi* written by Zhuangzi calls for losing oneself entirely in the Dao to achieve a transcendent self. In this way, liberation is reached through a higher source. All this to say, Confucianism and Daoism both call for a sincere loss of oneself to sacrifice for a higher power, which ultimately calls for personal agency and action. The motivation behind that agency can be considered "individualistic," but it is eventually built on surrendering and meeting religious obligations. Perhaps, the yin and yang within Asian culture are balancing the will to sacrifice and the selfish hunger for self-transcendence. Either way, the spiritual act embraces the Dalai Lama's message to find personal liberation, balance, and peace amid the noise and overwhelming public opinion (Brindley 2023).

While living in Taiwan, and after receiving a lot of information from Fulbright officials, I realized that students and parents stress that junior high success leads to admission into a great college, which leads to a great job and career. This horrific cycle of pressure causes increased stress levels and cortisol in Taiwanese students and Asian culture. This high pressure is exemplified in what the Taiwanese community calls "cram schools," where students can get ahead with more hours of high-intensity learning. This relentless push by parents and significant undying focus on careerism to continue the legacy of one's family is directly contrasted by tai chi's beautiful principles of calmness, connectedness, and holistic body and mental engagement.

In his 2016 video "The Physiology of Tai Chi and QiGong," Doctor Roger Jahnke explains that in America, performance is primarily thought to result from an anatomical function or "functionality." However, in Asia, the function is only one aspect of the body, called "chi." What is powerful, however, is the ability for function to increase due to practicing tai chi, which can empower and strengthen tai chi. Jahnke explains that "chi," or the energy emitted from "tai chi," finds its way into the middle of all your bones and is stored for "healing and empowerment" to handle Earth's gravity while bone marrow creates red and white blood cells. Ultimately, because the human body has bones throughout its frame, "chi" is omnipresent (Jahnke 2016).

"Chi" and blood function together. The activity of the blood in a relaxed state of practice is to feel blood circulate through your entire body and provide oxygen to all of your body. In other words, awareness of your flowing blood is about fluid chi. Fluid chi is like water moving over rocks in a stream. Within the lymphatic system, the chi is a fluid-based internal sensation. The lymph node is the internal waste eliminator and the immune cell delivery system, which acts like a big garbage truck inside your body, removing unneeded material.

Tai chi is said to enhance the propulsion of all these bodily fluids besides blood. Tai chi improves the chemistry of the nervous system and the complete network of neurons that help induce feelings and moods. The nervous system is like an electrical map of the body, powering and controlling the interworking of your body's senses. The organs are the center point for all chi interactivity, like the buildings and skyscrapers of a large city, housing and empowering workers like blood. The chi represents the chemistry between all the body's chemicals (hormones, nutrients, enzymes). Chi (life force energy) helps bring balance to the body's systems, and tai chi and qigong greatly assist with this balance, especially in our high-pressured society (Jahnke 2016).

When practiced correctly with the proper intention, tai chi creates a relaxation response by activating the parasympathetic nervous system and its healing hormones and inhibiting the sympathetic nervous system and its action hormones, such as inflammation. The parasympathetic nervous system is utilized for relaxation, digestion, rest, and recovery. This system is necessary for slowing down in today's overworked world. On the other hand, the sympathetic nervous system is often labeled the "fight or flight" system as it is utilized in high-stress situations like immediate action, eating a lot of food, or working out at the gym.

Because these tense situations may lead us to put more pressure on ourselves than we should, we often have poor physical reactions like a flushed face, over sweating, or even inflammation. I usually use this system because I am often on the go, trying to understand the different aspects of my life better while constantly trying to learn. I have been able to activate the parasympathetic nervous system more recently because I regularly get full body massages to relax my body and mind, creating powerful ripple effects for my "chi" or life force energy. Chi allows us to connect to ourselves throughout our whole bodies and the universe, as the "totality" of chi is the energy that makes up every human and the planet (Jahnke 2016).

Anoushka Veljee is head of product design for creARTme, a company founded to advocate for mindfulness in our increasingly stressed-out world. Interestingly, like the symbol of tai chi, evoking balance through art, Veljee utilizes art to harness a newfound sense of mindfulness in her students and the people she teaches in her workshops. Veljee understands that personal energy and how we use this energy can change how we move. Veljee explains that we must connect with ourselves to harness our energy within the world. This requirement is because art helps us reflect on the planet and determine why we are here and what we truly want for ourselves—allowing creators to ask themselves, "Why?" Aligning our goals with our desires and skills allows our "chi" to flow freely in the world while giving us true intentional momentum forward.

Veljee references Pablo Picasso's sentiment never to leave your inner child and innate creativity as you get older and most likely more risk averse. She declares:

> Art has the ability to express our innermost feelings and landscape and it truly goes beyond words. Art mindfulness as I see it is simple. It is about the process rather than the product.

I believe the tai chi or yin-yang symbol is an artful representation of mindfulness and what it means to be truly balanced. The black represents infinite possibilities for infinity, denoting liveliness, action, perseverance, and grittiness. The white represents endless possibilities that venture on forever, too, denoting stillness, reserve, silence, and restfulness. The colors expand the scope of imagination for what balance can be depending on the situation, allowing for its openness to fit anyone's situation based on their circumstances.

The artfulness of the symbol mirrors the craftiness of tai chi. According to the Tai Chi Institute, while performing tai chi correctly, "[m]ovements are fluid, graceful, circular and slow. Breathing is deep, aiding visual and mental concentration. This activity relaxes the body and allows the life force to flow freely" (Lam 2022). Like a painting, the flow of tai chi is like a paintbrush creating brush strokes: composed, elegant, and utilizing energy efficiently and effectively.

One November weekend, I decided to visit a Tai Chi Institution in downtown Magong to practice my tai chi and connect to my inner self on a deeper level. I walked through the beautiful Magong Zhongyang Old Street to find a tai chi place with an older man and two young students. I watched them practice their tai chi, and they seemed advanced for their age. In their white robes, they did high kicks and air punches before returning to standing positions with their hands together.

I noticed a definite shift in my spirit as I watched them. I became calmer and more collected. The energy they were omitting was peaceful and joyous. I could sense that the "chi" in the room was on a high level and vibrating at this high level consistently. I recognized that "chi" is similar to body heat in that it manifests stronger when several people contribute to the collective.

As the Dalai Lama alludes to in his teachings, finding peace derives from achieving balance. This sense of balance and stability arrives when "chi" is flowing freely throughout one's body, connecting one to oneself as well as with the rest of the world, where individualism and collectivism are the same, parallel to how "chi" represents the energy within each of us and all of us. Tai chi is important because it perpetuates centrality and wholeness while getting rid of pent-up stress or aggression that is undoubtedly disadvantageous to hold onto.

CHAPTER 4

Rich Spirit: Taoism (Daoism), Buddhism, Confucianism, and Christianity

---

"Life is a series of natural and spontaneous changes. Don't resist them; that only creates sorrow. Let reality be reality. Let things flow naturally forward in whatever way they like."
—*LAO TZU*

I read Lao Tzu's words multiple times, sitting in my comfy office chair after school lunch. I was nearing sleep because I was somewhat exhausted from the day before, which involved scootering around the islands of Penghu and a Chinese class at Penghu National University. I was looking for interesting Asian poems to read to pique my interest. I then came across several by Lao Tzu, also known as Lao Tse, Laotze, Laosi, and Laocius. Specifically, I came across many of his writings from

Tao Te Ching, credited with developing Taoism or Daoism, a religion that sprouted in Asia. Many consider it the founding document of Daoism to help followers follow the Dao.

That sentiment by Lao Tzu hit me hard. I read that multiple times because I usually kick myself over not following through or making small mistakes here and there. I grew up a chronic perfectionist, which generally caused me to remain stagnant or be afraid to do anything if it was not perfect. This sentiment put me at ease and reminded me about how short-lived life is, meaning that nothing should be overly planned and anything worth doing should be done and completed without overthinking or overdoing anything. The best products are created spontaneously and authentically, representing who you are and what you truly desire. Allow time to tell your natural story.

Lao Tzu and I would have been great homies because he advocated for nature, peace, and going with the flow. According to Cognito's 2020 YouTube video "Taoism Explained," Daoism is an indigenous Chinese religion. Still, it is not the sole majority, as several people in Asia practice a combination of Confucianism, Buddhism, and Daoism. Daoism emerged from the Warring States Period when many philosophers became famous (Amadeus 2020).

One such philosopher was Laozi. He talked about a force called Dao, which stands alone without changing. This concept is similar to what meditators call equanimity (Amadeus 2020).

Dao means "the way." Similar to "chi" or "qi," the "Dao" controls the universe, surrounding and existing around us. Laozi acknowledges that change is the only constant. The goal is to see "Dao" in the world and do nothing by force but through nature. To move with the "Dao," you must leave inflexible and structured circumstances to move freely with the "Dao" (Amadeus 2020).

The Daoists see yin and yang as an order as people grow up, age, and die. This cycle resembles how a plant grows from the ground up, loses its petals, and dies. Its original meaning was thought of when contemplating how the sun rises and shines a light on one side of a mountain and then moves to the other, shining light on that side.

According to a 2013 TEDEd video by John Bellaimey, "Daoists believe that the universe is made of energies, vibrations, and matter, which behave differently in different contexts." For instance, a wave includes yang in its crest and yin in its trough. The brake in a car is yin, and the gas pedal is yang. The eggshell is yang, and the egg within is yin. Yang starts the action, and yin receives it or completes it. For example, a pitch is yang, and a catch is yin. The back and the top of a person are the yang. Daoism or Taoism specifically stresses a more significant "force" rather than a greater "God" in the universe:

"It is higher, deeper, and truer than any other force. They call it the Tao. It means the way" (Bellaimey 2013).

Bellaimey elucidates that rather than yin and yang being rivals or competitive forces in the world, Daoism teaches that people must learn from both sides and follow the universe's natural guidance without fighting. Some principles mean listening more than arguing, being okay with going backward, and not worrying about being the best. Wise people are flexible and live simple, effortless lives.

Therefore, the light and dark sides change like a cycle controlled by the orbits around the sun. This cycle epitomizes how nothing stays the same; change is the only constant. "Qi," pronounced like "chi" in English, means "air" in Chinese. Qi refers to the energy that makes up the world (Amadeus 2020).

Qi flows through your body and keeps you alive. It is said that meditating, breathing, eating healthy, and overall self-care can bring about positive qi, which can help you live longer. Daoists see the heavens, the earth, and the body as reflections of each other, mirroring and affecting each other because the universe is one interrelated part (Amadeus 2020).

Several people associate Daoism with breathing and exercise, and tai chi is the trailblazer of that label. Officially, Tai chi is short for "Taiji Quan" or "boxing of the great ultimate." Tai chi is supposed to meet external forces with softness to redirect it. Several people, especially older people or stationary individuals, do noncombat tai chi, a slowed-down version meant to stimulate blood circulation and relaxation (Amadeus 2020). Bones, skin, flesh, and overall physical well-being are highly relevant to tai chi because they make up our energy and what we emit to the greater world, allowing us to connect and feel.

TAOISM (DAOISM): GODS, SPIRITS, GHOSTS, AND DEMONS

Daoism contains gods, and Chinese religion has many local deities, gods, spirits, and ghosts (Amadeus 2020).

According to Britannica, San-Ch'ing (Chinese for "Three Pure Ones") is considered the highest triad of deities within Daoism. During the T'ang Dynasty, the three deities were associated with the three highest heavens, also believed to be the "pure realms" in Taoism. Today, the deities are identified as "Original Beginning Heavenly Worthy," "Numinous Jewel Heavenly Worthy," and "Its Power Heavenly Worthy" or "Grand Lord Lao." In Taoism today, these deities are represented during "Chiao."

While in Taiwan, I sometimes saw religious deities represented within parades on the street or in puppet shows put on by my school, dressed or decorated as celestial animals, kings, or queens with bright colors. There is a unique energy and attention when recreating heavenly spirits; Taiwanese art does this a lot (The Editors of Encyclopaedia Britannica 2009).

For instance, according to a 2009 *Taipei Times* article, Huang Yo-Chien is a traditional temple painter based in Penghu County, a vital county in a country home to the highest density of religious buildings in all of Taiwan. The county is also my home for a year. Incredibly, 70 percent of the temples in Penghu are covered with his paintings, and most of his paintings are "door gods": bright, colorful, and beaming with facial personalities, portraying beautiful embodiments of spirituality. He has made a career of over sixty years, painting gods on doors and walls. In Penghu alone, he has over two hundred temples featuring his characters (Wu 2009).

Because of his word contributions, Scholars widely label Laozi as the founder of Daoism. However, Zhang Daoling contributed a lot to Daoism because of the revelation he received from Lord Lao. He wanted to mirror the bureaucracy of gods in heaven on earth, so he created The Way of the Celestial Masters. This creation was the birth of groups practicing Daoism (Amadeus 2020).

Laozi ascended to godhood and is now called "Lord Lao." He is considered an incarnation of the "Dao." There are other gods for every need, such as demons, marriage problems, or examinations (Amadeus 2020). According to a 2023 Owlcation article, Taoism, sometimes referred to as China's "indigenous faith," like Buddhism, has many gods that were influenced by classical literature and went through multiple phases or transformations. For instance, Erlang Shen, a unique three-eyed Taoist deity, was once known as the god of agriculture and is now known as a warrior deity due to classical novels expressing him in that way (Yong 2023).

Another unique Taoist god story involves Xi Wang Mu, or "The Queen Mother of the West." She started as an ancient Chinese mother goddess and then was placed into Taoism and became associated with "immortality" and "longevity." Many believe the heavenly woman lives in Kun Lun or the "mythical mountain range of Taoism." Most gods become associated with an idea or an avenue for a specific opportunistic outcome.

I remember growing up and losing things quite often. I was even humorously voted "Most likely to win the lottery and lose the ticket" in my high school yearbook. My grandmother often prayed to Saint Sebastian to help find the missing item. Taoist gods are similar to Christian Saints but have a different mythical quality due to ancient Chinese mythology and bright Asian iconography and symbolism. Another Taoist God is Dou Mu Niang Niang, or "the mother goddess of The Big Dipper stars." Initially, however, she was worshiped by the ancient Chinese as the creator of all the stars and constellations (Yong 2023).

Daoism is a very conceptual religion based on the work of Laozi, so it is practiced in many forms. I have witnessed several Taiwanese practice Daoism in Buddhist and Confucianism temples as Asian spirituality is often very fluid between the three, such as meditation and finding inner healing while respecting elders.

The yin and yang symbol has, therefore, naturally bled through Daoism into the other Asian religions that may be more popular such as Buddhism. I have seen the yin-yang symbol on the walls of Buddhist temples, Confucian temples, and folk temples (a combination of Buddhism and Taoism with a Confucian worldview). The cyclical symbol representing an unending paradoxical and diametric movement is a staple in most Asian religious contexts and can arguably be applied to many religious values worldwide.

According to a 2021 BBC article, "Why Do Buddhists Meditate?" a follower of Buddhism aspires to be awakened like the Buddha. To reach this enlightenment, people must achieve a specific mental state through meditation and mindfulness. The Tibetan meditation tradition utilizes a mantra, which is repeated to help focus the mind and epitomize Kanjur, or the words of the Buddha. The Theravada tradition asks followers to focus on breath, body, or mental images rather than words (BBC Teach 2021).

The classic Buddha pose, as many Americans have seen via giant golden statues in restaurants or cultural centers, features the Buddha with a balanced upper body, crossed legs, and hands gently balanced on his lap. This posture usually allows comfortability (the ultimate goal while meditating) to focus on breath and reach a state of renewal, recharge, and clarity. This powerfully transcendental meditation fully engages the chest and diaphragm for airflow, where enlightenment can be discovered (BBC Teach 2021).

My journey to "enlightenment," or what I deem as awareness of self, the world, and others, was anything but smooth. Growing up, I never had to worry about my next meal or where I would go home at night. Because of my financial security, I was often reckless, unafraid to drink, test relationships, try different drugs, and host parties at my family home. I was absorbed with the thought of just having fun all the time.

Meditation or thinking about my intentions was never on my constantly racing mind. Instead, I always seemed distracted by people, places, and new beginnings being thrown at me all the time. Trying many different things was very important while growing up. I dipped my toes in many other pools: campus ministry, student government, football, baseball, basketball, volleyball, and advanced placement courses. In college, I served as an undergraduate student body senator, got involved in the Christian ministry, participated in Greek Life, played several intramural sports, and accepted an invitation to join the Warren Bennis Leadership Cohort in his honor. While doing a lot is excellent, I never felt "enlightened" until I stopped momentarily to take a breath and develop my relationship with God.

The moment I was baptized in the Pacific Ocean at Santa Monica, declaring that "Jesus is Lord" and my attachment to nondenominational Christianity, my journey to awareness began.

I felt refreshed and clean. All the work, pain, and mistakes I'd made until that point were to mold me into a man ready to take on the world after college and raise a family with a wife and kids. February 13, 2021, was a memorable day in my life, when I came to terms with the idea that I was enough and will always be sufficient. God understands me and my restless, chaotic energy.

This moment, also during the pandemic, taught me how to slow down, how to reflect, and how to live intentionally. Until then, I had never carried out this "living intentionally" idea. My church and residing in my hometown during the pandemic taught me that every moment is critical in my life, not just because it is under God's watchful eyes but because time is precious, and my years are not something I can get back.

Meditation became a state of mind for me in 2021, allowing me to revamp my life. No longer was I entrenched with the need for external validation. No longer was I living mindlessly, simply looking for fun or an escape. No longer was I unintentional. My life was *always on purpose.*

This purposefulness started with my spirituality and reading scriptures in the Bible to live a life like Jesus Christ: standing up for those who needed it, serving those who deserved it, spreading love, and loving my enemies just as much as my friends. My life became a soft haze where I felt productive, and my life became meaningful, fruitful, and beautiful in so many more ways.

Doctor Varun Soni is one of my favorite teachers of all time, and he has an office in the USC Office of Religious and Spiritual Life (ORSL). Varun is a Hindu, and his spirituality has bled a lot into my Christian faith.

Specifically, Soni has taught me values that reinforce what Biblical texts preach, such as valuing happiness over greed, connection over persecution, genuineness over judgment, and realness over sugar-coated bliss.

My faith has brought me a newfound sense of authentic confidence and a quiet poise that will forever allow me to live with purpose and protection. Like Christianity, any religion creates a solid foundation for its followers regardless of the differing definition of gods or higher beings. Furthermore, this stable reassurance establishes a balance in my life. Every moment I am awake, I perform at my highest level. Every time I sleep, I achieve the best sleep filled with REM. Like Daoists and Buddhists, I earn a level of inner peace.

CONFUCIANISM: AS IT RELATES TO TAOISM

Asia Society explains that Confucianism differs from Daoism, Buddhism, and Christianity because it is a philosophy rather than a religion. Because of this, many Daoists and Buddhists have a worldview encompassing Confucianism principles. Under Han Emperor Wu in 140 BCE, Confucianism became accepted as "state ideology and orthodoxy." Confucian values were seen to promote structure in society and the status quo. The education system and emperors rewarded citizens who embodied Confucian values: respecting elders, government loyalty, and performing one's duty in society. However, Confucianism also pushed for the practice of "ren," or humaneness and love. The Chinese character for the word denotes a relationship between "two persons." "Ren" is similar to yin and yang because it symbolizes two entities unionizing in harmony. Both concepts are about a solid and meaningful two-sided balanced relationship that perpetuates what humaneness truly means—unconditional and undying connectivity (Berling 2023).

Ren, like meditation, allows one to heal from within by helping to develop a solid inner ethical character.

As exemplified by the emphasis on self-reflection and self-awareness within three prominent Asian religions and my religion, it is clear that the conceptual meaning of the yin and yang symbol can be applied to spiritual practice. Meditation and reaching a point of equanimity benefit anyone flourishing within their religious community by spreading their faith or living out their faith's principles.

Those who follow a religion, no matter what it is, who also strive for equanimity are following yin and yang aspects. Sometimes, thinking less translates into becoming more of who you are. Sometimes, speaking less allows you to listen and learn more. Whether eating sushi in Japan or walking the shores of Mexico City during sunset, slowing down to take some time to be intentional will always help you understand where you are and where you want to go, allowing you to enhance the complementary forces within yourself.

CHAPTER 5

Mirrors...

———

"Light and shadow are opposite sides of the same coin. We can illuminate our paths or darken our way. It is a matter of choice."
—MAYA ANGELOU

There has always been a mirror on the wall in every room I have ever had. In my childhood home in Los Gatos, California, the entire front of my closet was a mirror, reflecting my whole room to me with me as the inhabitant. In Taiwan, the rooms I have lived in on the archipelago have mirrors, a point to center myself and check myself—a metaphor for life and a peek into my soul. When I look into my mirrors, I always look for two important things: my eyes and my mouth. I can tell if I am tired, sad, happy, or enthusiastic when I peer into my eyes. I hope to see my teeth and a broad smile when I look at my mouth. It is a reflection of reality and a challenge to accept my current state whether I like it or not.

We cannot change who we are. We can only accept ourselves and grow accordingly. As Michael Jackson voiced in his tenth number-one single, "Man in the Mirror," we all must begin by looking at who we are and what we genuinely desire to recharge our lives.

We must realize that the greatest obstacle in our lives is often us. We assume barriers exist when they do not. We think people watch or judge us when they could not care less. We place so much pressure on ourselves when everything will always work out.

Look in the mirror, and love what you see while taking it in. Make the most of what you can with this life while under-standing that you are loved and understood by those who matter to you, and you never have to prove anything. You have to exist and, through this, find balance within yourself. What you are meant to do and who you are meant to be will reveal itself.

Jun Shan, PhD, president of Csymbol.com and ArtChops, explained that the yin-yang symbol illustrates duality, para-dox, unity in diversity, change, and harmony. Not many signs can simultaneously represent many of life's great necessities (2020).

According to a May 16, 2018 article by Mark Cartwright in World History Encyclopedia, the study of Yin and Yang, par-ticularly this idea of two opposing forces, became popular with the work of the Chinese school called Yingyang, whose studies sprouted in the third Century BCE. The creator or pusher of this profound theory was cosmologist Zou Yan (or Tsou Yen), who believed that life went through five phases:

fire, water, metal, wood, and earth. These phases continuously change as both yin and yang change (Cartwright 2018).

Yin represents darkness, femininity, and passivity.

This energy entails:
- blackness
- coldness
- even numbers
- valleys
- water
- the moon
- north
- soft
- old
- Earth (Cartwright 2018).

Yin, especially in my life today, comes in pure rest: taking important naps, reading in bed while remaining stationary, and allowing my food to digest fully. I often will hit roadblocks or periods of extreme fatigue due to being overworked or simply because my body tells me I need relaxation. This aspect of yin in my life is such a necessary element within my lifestyle because it allows me to recuperate, decompress, and get ready for an event that may be extreme or daring.

Yang represents light, masculinity, and action.

This energy entails:
- whiteness
- warmness
- odd numbers

- mountains
- fire
- the sun
- south
- hard
- young
- Heaven (Cartwright 2018).

Yang shows up when I confidently chase a goal or joyfully have fun with my friends while drinking a beer. I think in that moment one truly sees the light inside oneself while recognizing one's gifts. This recognition can be equated to yang's warmness to self or yang's fire within.

The constant change in the relationship between these two poles is responsible for the constantly changing state of the universe and life itself. When the balance is too much, the world can enter disastrous circumstances through mother nature's wrath (Cartwright 2018). Like Earth's inevitable end in the future, this imbalance mirrors and demonstrates how humans are out of balance with the Earth. We consistently hurt the planet through carelessness, which involves not throwing trash away properly or misusing the Earth's resources.

As a human race, we must learn to balance ourselves. Then we can begin to balance our relationship with our planet.

I have witnessed this exciting and necessary mirror of existence in Taiwan—the dark web always exists beneath the real web. For instance, beneath the friendliness and happy exterior of faces and interaction lies a real and highly stressed-out need to make a living for oneself. Several workers at my school have to forgo families to work and provide for themselves. I see kids trying to get ahead in cram schools, pushed to be someone through rushing through learning.

As I was making my way up to my apartment on the fourth floor next to Beichen Market, one of Penghu's most popular morning markets, a boy was standing alone outside his door on the third floor. He looked helpless and tired. I asked him what he was waiting for before inviting him to come to my apartment without receiving any answer.

He had come home from cram school, and his parents were not home yet. I ushered him to our couch, where he started to do his math homework. He was programmed to work nonstop without taking a break. He stayed for about an hour, working the whole way through, before leaving to return home. Many students possess this impeccable drive to out-compete others.

In Silicon Valley, where I am from in the United States, competition in school is constantly at an all-time high. It is so hard to continuously out-compete your classmates all the time. I feel this educational system in America represents the yin-yang contrast because although there are fantastic teachers, there remains a lot of "gaming the system" or cheating to get the best grades to enter a great college.

Like the yin-yang symbol, this is paradoxical because the competition in the first place drives students to forgo natural learning while enjoying the process instead of focusing on studying correctly or cheating, in other words, focusing on the highest possible amount of inaction (yin) to maintain still the highest amount of results and recognition (yang).

Of course, we need rest and action to be our best selves, but working to rest is not beneficial. Instead, we must understand that rest is to fulfill our life's valuable purpose to impact those around us in our particular field or domain. Essentially, the symbol unwinds, and the universe's many twists and turns come to intention. Intention adds meaning to choices. Living an intentional life is the key to opening up a life of mindfulness, balance, and peace. The only way to find this intention is by unwinding yourself and fully exposing yourself for you, the world, and God to witness.

DARKNESS AND LIGHT: WORKING TOGETHER TO INFORM OUR LIVES
When looking into a mirror, we may see the ugly and haunting parts of ourselves and the world. Because of that darkness, trauma, disrespect, and sabotage (both personal and external), we can contribute light, action, progress, and servitude to the world. We must do this to survive and balance out what too much sleep or darkness can do to us.

According to a 2022 Healthline article by Emily Swaim and Karin Gepp, PsyD, called "7 Reminders to Carry with You on Your Trauma Recovery Journey," trauma takes much time to heal from because there are five stages to get through. Recovering from trauma requires your whole self to be involved, and self-care can be a great outlet to protect yourself from the outside world. Therapy may also lend a helping hand, involving "emotional safety, cultural sensitivity, agency, and social connection." Patience is essential, but deliberate and relentless action is also necessary to overcome the hump. When we work on our trauma, the light can come into our lives. Sometimes, the light comes in little pinpoints at first or in subtle ways until we can find our true selves again. Daring to face and heal your trauma makes more healthy yang possible—the fulfilling sense of taking action from a more refreshed, renewed place (Swaim 2022).

In life, we sometimes feel guilty for not delivering to everyone we know and disappointing those who count on us. All we can do is our best and just be ourselves. I have struggled sometimes throughout my life, feeling like I always need to help those around me. This feeling comes from a desire to make the world a better place and to please my friends in every way possible. For instance, I would go out of my way to help my housemates move their furniture into our house, or I would do all of my brother's homework without being asked. I think knowing people need my help makes me feel valuable.

Undoubtedly, it is critical to develop awareness of this unneeded compulsive trait to always put others before ourselves. It began with looking at myself in the mirror and understanding what I wanted out of life. I realize my drive to serve comes from my compassionate nature and love for putting a smile on people's faces. Whether through charity work or teaching, serving will always be a part of my life.

Humans must realize that we are put on this planet to bring our gifts to the world.

Inevitably, there will be low points where this ability is hindered due to roadblocks. We must surround ourselves with people who challenge, engage, and lift us up. We should not surround ourselves with people who are jealous of us, constantly take from us, or do not serve us in any way.

When we start to feel unserved or uninspired, we must leave the situation and create a group that challenges us to think differently while bringing out the best in ourselves.

WHAT IT MEANS TO BE A GENTLE WARRIOR

I do not believe in constantly changing ourselves for our surroundings to make others feel more comfortable at our expense. If you cannot be authentic while remaining respectful to the people you are with, achieving balance may be challenging. From what I have learned about yin and yang, achieving balance is an ongoing pursuit to live gracefully and fully.

On the last day of November 2022, I scootered to my office quickly in a misty haze, enveloping the city of Magong at just 6:30 in the morning. I woke up at 4 a.m. for a vanilla latte from 7-Eleven, so I was wide awake for my 7 a.m. chat with Michael McDonald.

McDonald is different from the usual bald and bright businessman. He greeted me with a warm smile and introduced me to his cat. Nothing feels forced. He founded his own coaching company named after himself, helping transform entrepreneurs and executives by inspiring them to reach a higher consciousness—something I do daily. I related to McDonald because of the self-proclaimed way he engages life as a "gentle warrior-philosopher": a dualistic oxymoron in its own right. Gentleness is essential to appreciate life's little moments, but being a warrior is critical to staying curious.

Interestingly, when chatting about light and darkness, McDonald admitted that he does not often use these terms. Still, he does think about darkness in his shadow work. To him, darkness and light are connected to the state of being hidden and noticed. He tries to teach his clients to stop negatively reacting when discovering more about themselves.

The important lesson is to find the light within as one becomes more authentic continuously. It is being able to look at yourself in the mirror and accept whatever you are looking at wholeheartedly.

McDonald and I agreed that sitting with insecurities, pasts, and worries without trying to fix anything or consistently reacting allows whatever needs healing within those concepts to heal with time and patience.

McDonald distinguished between two types of mindfulness: deliberate and effortless.

My mindfulness is usually effortless as I try to remain in a state of calmness and equanimity at all times. Striving to be a gentle warrior means reaching a state where my mindfulness is effortless, and my actions are deliberate. This intentionality and precision means finding purpose in every step I take. When running or jogging in life, metaphorically, I see a consistent rhythm where my goals, feelings, and vision match beautifully. Sometimes, I move too fast instead of taking one step at a time, putting me in different unfortunate pickles. It is crucial to continue growing and moving on. However, it is vital to slow down and remain patient so things within your life can work out how they should.

I will deliberately push myself to reach a state of relaxation through intentional mindfulness meditations in the morning or at night. Interestingly, McDonald believed that looking down and seeing others with low consciousness is easy. Still, looking up and understanding those with high consciousness is very hard. The more I think about it, the more this makes sense, as the more in the moment one is, the easier it is to control oneself while also reaching awareness in those around them. The act of looking into the mirror truthfully allows us to accept who is there while also acknowledging the people and places around us while away from the mirror to reflect on our stance in that environment.

Sometimes noise can blur what we look like in the mirror, making us appear worse or not like how we are. To reach a state of peace and an existence of effortlessness, we must come to differentiate outside noise and our inside signal. Subtracting noise allows us to step fully into our self-portrait.

In his 2022 film, *Stutz,* Jonah Hill introduces his therapist to the world, Doctor Phil Stutz. After introducing loads of tools and ideologies, Stutz pushes Hill to be vulnerable and open up about the shame he felt when he was younger and overweight. Stutz explains the concept of our "shadow": the version of ourselves that we dislike and want to hide from the outside world. However, Stutz reasons that everyone must discover their shadow and work with it to be a whole and healthy person. By acknowledging and loving our shadow, we present, communicate, date, and perform better in high-stakes events. It is about being content inside your skin and tolerating whatever may happen in your life. Stutz explains, "The idea of being in sync with the shadow…it's a sense of wholeness. Wholeness means I don't need anything else. 'I am whole the way I am.' And that's very freeing" (Hill 2022).

When we are connected and rooted in all of ourselves (the good, the bad, and the ugly), it is easier to connect to the world because we feel whole and are less likely to engage in destructive actions. Accepting our shadow is an act of self-love, vulnerability, and realness. It may be challenging, but it allows us to feel the full spectrum of our emotions and needs by paying attention to all of who we are.

Ultimately, how one feels and that powerful sense of personal balance returns to grounding, essentially connected to spirituality. Being aligned with oneself and one's goals allows one to have integrity and be content even in times of chaos, pitch blackness (darkness), or extreme exposure (lightness). Undoubtedly, it is our choice to illuminate our paths or to work on our shadows—to degrade ourselves and others while going down a dark road or to shine who we are authentically.

The latter enables us to see ourselves clearly in the mirror to take action with intention. Living chaotically and mindlessly can unintentionally lead us to drag ourselves through the mud. We do not always need to live on a clear-cut schedule, but we need an idea of where we want to go and what we want to do. Maintaining a clear sense of personality and loose lifetime strategy will allow us to thrive and grow while remaining flexible.

CHAPTER 6

The Crippling Workaholic Tradition: Never Sleep

THE ASIAN AND AMERICAN TRADITIONS

"Choose a job you love, and you will never have to work a day in your life."
—CONFUCIUS

I often do not sleep. Not because I do not want to but simply because life will make me too excited to want to escape the action. Action is fun for me. Work is fun for me. But several people have labeled me as a "workaholic." Workaholic has a very negative connotation. It is not a label one should strive for, yet it is often attributed to some of the greatest champions in our world. I struggle with letting go of my ideas and doing nothing.

I am always thinking, always dreaming, and always plotting. I also tend to overthink, constantly deciphering what should be enhanced in my life and why I may have forgotten it earlier. This bad habit often makes me my worst enemy, lost in my head, and highly self-critical.

Doctor Ramani Durvasula explains on an episode of her groundbreaking podcast called *Navigating Narcissism* that overworking can even be a form of dissociation. She acknowledges in "Confronting Complex PTSD with Stephanie Foo" that even though we fetishize people who can work around the clock, it can be a sign of dissociation from reality—an avenue to detach from feeling and living in the present moment. In this way, work acts as a barrier to self-acceptance and appreciation. I think several workaholics are guilty of this, as work serves as a drug of escapism rather than a healthy means of discovering or making a living. Whatever the reason for working too much may be, it is essential to take breaks to reassure that your drive is, in fact, a healthy one and not an unhealthy one (Durvasula 2023).

Sometimes, we can act or work compulsively without acknowledging the personal subconscious feelings that may drive us. For instance, last week, I felt myself constantly burying the lurking rumination inside my brain regarding my previous book and everything I could have done differently in curating it. I became angry and stressed because I drove myself down that path. This dangerous never-ending perfectionist game ultimately gets me nowhere and leads to agony and more overworking to avoid giving myself the space to feel or think about the past. It is essential to accept the past, whether it may be good or bad in our eyes, and not let a workaholic tradition be a form of disassociation or an attempt to forget our current state at rest.

I am getting better at this.

In Chinese religion, Confucianists favor yang or action as the primary focus within their ideologies. Confucianists believe engagement in life is significant for meaning and purpose. This emphasis means that inherently workers are stressed to outperform their opponents and to overextend themselves.

Confucius suggests that finding a job that becomes more of a hobby is a solution to the Confucian ideal that work is a significant priority in society. The fact that this is a thought points to the commonly held worldly belief that your "job" is extremely important.

In the book, *The Political Economy of Business Ethics in Asia: A Historical and Comparative Perspective* (2017), authors Baumann and Winzar introduce the ReVaMB Model. This detailed model outlines the relational values of Confucianism as well as the behavior of Confucian determination in the workplace. Within this chapter, I will dive deep into relative values, workplace behavior, burnout, and moderating and antecedent factors from the ReVaMB Model.

RELATIVE VALUES: CHOOSE WORK YOU LOVE BECAUSE IT CARRIES IMMENSE WEIGHT

Delving into relative values, one significant Confucius value that encompasses several other Confucianism ideals is filial piety. According to chapter 5.5 ("Filial Piety in Changing

Asian Societies") in *The Cambridge Handbook of Age and Ageing* by Akiko Hashimoto and Charlotte Ikels, "Filial piety refers to the practice of respecting and caring for one's parents in old age, based on a moral obligation that children owe their parents." Because children feel they owe their parents, they naturally have an innate pressure as they go about their day to live up to expectations—the *expectation* to follow the rules, the *expectation* of earning incredibly high grades, and the *expectation* to exceed expectations.

Filial piety is what Americans call pride—finding strength in where you come from. Whereas Eastern culture often pressures children to perform well to carry on the family's legacy and contribute to society, Western culture repeatedly stresses being unique to break free from societal standards in an individualistic way to make a name for yourself. Success in Asia is usually predicated on one's ability to serve the community.

In contrast, in America, more success is more often attributed to those who stand out from the crowd for being significantly different, utilizing the skills and traits learned from their family. Filial piety is meant to constitute giving in the Asian context. At the same time, family in America is often used for a sense of pride and personal power to go out and achieve for yourself (Hashimoto and Ikels 2005).

WORKPLACE BEHAVIOR: CAREERISM'S NEED FOR SPEED

Another word in the "workplace behavior" column within the ReVaMB Model is "speed of work." This speediness often sets people apart, but it can also cause people to make brutal mistakes. The classic American Fable, "The Tortoise and the

Hare," teaches that slow and steady wins a race rather than unnerving quickness. Another theme of this story is that in life, it is always how one finishes, not how one starts. I have witnessed this speed of work aspect of Confucianism throughout my time in Taiwan (Baumann and Winzar 2017).

In the morning in Penghu, several scooterists honk and make their way through the market where all the fishermen set up their seafood, including oysters, sushi, groupers, and many more. Talking to my principal, Bruce, in English, I recognized that speeding to some finish line is always on the mind of the Taiwanese. He says he knows his kids have immense pressure. Still, he wants them to be able to live and have fun because he understands that life is incredibly short. You cannot possibly be perfect at every single possible thing. He says that because he loves seeing his students grow, and he greatly enjoys his job. Working in the school is his true passion, and he would not trade it for anything in the world because he truly understands what is best for kids—a holistic learning experience with primary subject homework, physical activity, cultural immersion, sports, arts, and international education. Like scooters racing through the farmers market, parents often want their students to run in their education, learning as much as they can to succeed in higher education and the professional field.

However, speed can also lead to burnout or extreme fatigue, creating a massive crater of inactivity because of the dire need for rest. Because I am obsessed with coffee and working out, I can escape burnout for some time. Still, it remains a barrier for me and all my American friends.

Several people I work with in Taiwan have gotten sick due to stress or being overworked. While working at my school, most teachers had to stay home many days or even a week because they were not feeling well. This break is undoubtedly brought about by overworking themselves and the immune system breaking down. Another factor is the undying COVID-19 pandemic plaguing my school on Penghu's southern peninsula. Either way, the stress is tangible in how people sometimes interact, with quivering or shaking voices in high-pressure situations or when speaking to someone new.

There is a fine line between laziness and restlessness. I enjoy being lazy as much as the next person and am considering the cost of lounging around. Conversely, it is crucial to understand whether all the energy we put into our work is genuinely worth it. That is why it is essential to find tranquility within this balance beam of yin and yang, where work does not feel like a chore but a fulfillment of our purpose. This quest is undoubtedly easier mentioned than performed.

According to *Psychology Today*, burnout involves emotional, mental, and physical exhaustion due to excessive constant stress. The triple threat of fatigue can be caused by many obligations that take away from self-care and self-identity. Also, working toward a seemingly unattainable goal with no sense of purpose or fulfillment often leads to burnout. The side effects of this horrendous phenomenon are tiredness, headaches, heart problems, and "feelings of anger, irritability, and cynicism." Stress is short-lived and caused by a single assignment or goal in mind, while burnout is long-lasting with deep feelings of sadness and hopelessness (Psychology Today Staff 2023).

At some point in our lives, we have felt a sense of burnout, whether from a toxic relationship, an unreasonable task, or seemingly pointless work. My first dose of burnout was during my sophomore year of high school when I lost my second grandmother. During football season, this tragedy left me not wanting to play while also trying to keep up with four honors classes in school and trying to meet others in the school. I could not handle the insurmountable pressure. I just wanted to sleep all the time, and I could barely get through my homework without passing out or thinking about death. The moment was dramatic. Burnout, which in this case was caused by grief and a loaded schedule, is like being knocked down by a tornado, hopeless at the hands of the windstorm, unable to stand back up and continue moving forward on a standard path.

EXTERNAL INPUTS: MODERATING AND ANTECEDENT

Of course, external factors affect how these values show up, such as moderating and antecedent factors.

Some moderating factors include workplace norms, organization type, and career stage. These factors are developed from the workplace culture (how the boss communicates and motivates his team and the company's purpose).

Antecedent factors are connected to one's family tree and the circumstance they are born into. For example, personality, family, and education are all antecedent factors in the ReVaMB model.

It is striking but unsurprising that the top three workplace behavior nouns are internal motivation, drive to perform, and drive to compete. This powerful trifecta at the top of the list screams high performance (Baumann and Winzar 2017).

WORKPLACE NORMS

According to *Forbes*, "[w]orkplace or team norms are usually defined as how team members interact, communicate, share, collaborate and coordinate." Norms can either aid or hinder a team from success frequently, and they constantly change due to the environment (Forbes Coaches Council 2022).

I sat in Montecarlo Cafe, hidden away in the middle of downtown Penghu. A picture of Santa with the words "Coffee and Tea" adorns the beautiful entrance with a quaint door and many plants. I walked in at 3:30 p.m. to a packed cafe with people working, talking, and enjoying each other's company this November 11 Saturday afternoon. Even on a Saturday without worrying about work, I gravitated toward researching the depths of different Asian religions, listening to informative podcasts, creating PowerPoints for school, or simply writing my thoughts. This urge is almost inescapable for me.

Coming from America, where I used to work all the time, including weekends, it is hard not to work on Saturdays. We have a common expectation to constantly check our emails and check off our to-do list every day of the week. Working on the weekends has always been a constant in my life because I have always had a goal or objective in my mind to get done for the following week. I often have been labeled a "workaholic." Still, I think many people in today's world are workaholics because career success is usually based on work ethic and experience. In the business world, whether on Wall Street or in Silicon Valley as an entrepreneur, working fast and often is essential to get ahead, earn a promotion, or move up the corporate ladder. Working hard or going home is often the workplace norm.

Both the United States and Taiwan have an emphasis on academics and work ethic. America may be more relaxed around workplace interaction, encouraging friendliness, first-name interactions, and smiling. I noticed that in Taiwan, maybe due to having English first names, most people do not address each other by their first names, and there is a lot more seriousness among the staff. There is rarely confrontation in a Taiwanese classroom, so directness is seldom appreciated. On the other hand, in America, frankness and honesty are usually expected at all times because the atmosphere is more collaborative and louder. At my school in Taiwan, I have realized most teachers are very independent and take care of their business without getting too involved in others' business.

According to the Center for Creative Leadership, a coaching workplace atmosphere has embedded coaching within its leadership and development structure, equips influential leaders with conversational skills, and demonstrates the value of coaching daily. In other words, coaching workplace culture is filled with encouragement, support, and full-on engagement. Being a leader within any community, especially in the mental health or spiritual space, is a job that requires patience, presence, and more importantly, complete understanding (Center for Creative Leadership 2022).

I grew up in Silicon Valley. This area in California is known for some of the biggest companies in the world, such as Meta, Apple, Google, LinkedIn, Adobe, and Zoom. Many consider this hub a hyperactive bubble of nonstop creation, molding its local workers into machines, stopping at nothing to instill greatness in the corporation they commit themselves to forever.

Growing up in this competitive hotbed of achievement, I felt pressure to do everything at the highest level possible nonstop; there was never a limit for me in terms of involvement. Unfortunately, I believed that the more I did or could juggle, the better off I would be. In Silicon Valley, this is often the mind-set. Ironically, as I sit in a cafe in Taiwan, Asia, I reflect on my time in Northern California, where most of my friends were Asian, the sons and daughters of immigrants coming for long careers in tech.

We pushed each other to complete lab reports, perform research for essays, and win games on the sports field. It was fun to push each other in new ways, but after every finals season, I would feel burned out. If I did not achieve perfect grades, I would also feel depressed. Growing up where I did, perfectionism manifested itself in everything I did. If my projects or creations were imperfect, I beat myself up for days on end. It was a disgusting habit that I and many of my high-achieving friends had, tirelessly working to be the best version of ourselves we possibly could. I ended up all right, but I have thankfully given up this ideal of perfectionism. At least, I think. The first thing I will tell my kids will be to let go of it. Just relax because everything will happen as it should without force. Relaxing is rooted in the yin aspect of yin yang, and going with the flow is related to the way of the Tao, letting nature take its due course.

I enjoy getting massages to find balance amid many antecedent factors in my life. After visiting my favorite cafe on the island, I strolled to the local massage place. I frequently visited the Four Points Sheraton Hotel Spa to get full-body back massages in August, September, and October. Massages, for me, are therapy. I found a new spot in the downtown streets of Magong City, Penghu County, the capital of Penghu.

On this day, I asked the gentleman, who knew me very well at this point as a regular, for a sixty-minute foot massage (liùshí). As I sat, listening to a Service95 podcast, I was content with the fact that perhaps a life in Asia forever would not be a bad thing. Prices were a lot cheaper (one US dollar equated to thirty-one Taiwanese dollars), and what I had seen up until that point featured so much peace. For once, away from my hometown and done with school and strict deadlines for the first time, I realized that not working all the time had finally given me a sense of personal security and inner peace like never before.

I was not racing with anyone but myself. I was no longer a cog in a system. I was simply a human being floating in existence on Earth, just being me. And that was magical.

CHAPTER 7

Spiritual Transcendence: Islas Pescadores

—

"May your dreams not come true."
—SADHGURU

The islands of Penghu, a beautiful and windy tropical archipelago off the west coast of Taiwan, have been labeled the Islas Pescadores by the Portuguese, describing the many fishermen on the island. Immediately, as I acclimated to life in Magong City—the largest city in the set of ninety islands and islets—I noticed large amounts of fish everywhere I looked. Because I lived next to a market, every morning starting at 5 a.m., fishermen would prepare their fish to be bought by locals walking by.

It became my routine to wake up every morning before scootering to school to walk through this beautiful kaleidoscope of colorful seafood—from oysters and shrimp to sushi and full-body groupers (the most popular fish on the island). Watching butchers work so hard to assemble what they caught fresh each morning was magical, entertaining, and other-worldly. Coming from California, I had never seen people work so hard so early in the morning. In my hometown of Los Gatos, California, my dad and I would always check out the local farmers market, but it was solely on Sundays, similar to the farmers markets in Los Angeles.

Beichen Market, the market I woke up to every morning, was a daily occurrence, serenading my adventurous spirit with vivid butchering, chattering, and the murmuring of "Nĭ hǎo" at every corner and crevice of the three-story market. In a gorgeous way, this energetic focus on fish and the market was a transcendent experience because it was orchestrated like a performance, leaving me in awe and gratitude. These water animals single-handedly created and inspired life throughout the city. The economy is mainly built on these underwater creatures. The culture was fascinating to me.

Second, I noticed convenient places of worship in several areas around harbors or fishing, whether a temple or a small hut. After speaking with many local fishermen, I understood that fishermen and religion were incredibly intertwined because fishermen continuously crafted deep relationships with God and prayed for fruitful fishing exploration each day, as this represented their livelihood. Their spirituality presents balance and beauty within their relatively physically demanding jobs. Without the escape of religion and scripture, fishermen would not have a beautiful counterpart to their hectic and inconsistent employment.

Once I settled into my day-to-day routine, I also realized that specific Taiwanese holidays were different from American holidays. These days provided an outlet for busy locals to celebrate their culture. The first one I experienced was called Moon Festival or Mid-Autumn Festival on September 10. On this holiday, I visited a local BBQ restaurant—a popular restaurant in Penghu, where you place food on a grill in the middle of your table—with my Fulbright cohort. During the day, I gave a presentation about the point of the holiday to a local Taiwanese elementary school, presenting sentences for them to finish with a verb. Participating in traditions was an excellent way to learn about Taiwanese culture and all it had to offer me. Once I realized that Taiwan had several holidays specific to its region, I could delve deeper into the culture, transcending into a new culture by paying attention.

My life in Asia was fun and challenging because of this new holiday schedule, forcing me to restructure the time map within my head. I fully immersed myself into this unique wild duality of Asia in my head—another physical island for exploration and the unfamiliar cultural aspects of Taiwan balanced with the life I was living in the United States (fifteen hours behind) and the American relationships I wanted to maintain. I was lounging in my office, working on a lesson plan for a shadow from the Fulbright shadow team the day after, when my Language English Teacher or LET (Merry or Yuwei Chang) and I chatted about the many unique days that made up the Asian calendar. Merry has lived in Taiwan her whole life and taught me a lot about the cultural aspects of the country.

First is Chinese New Year, which serves to celebrate the coming of the new year. For Chinese New Year, I stayed at the beautiful W Taipei, overlooking the busy Taipei 101 and downtown Taipei. As I walked around the capital of Taiwan with my parents, the buzz of the new year was very apparent. The city was gearing up for the Lantern Festival, celebrated on the Chinese calendar's fifteenth day of the first month. In 2023, it fell very early, on February 5, 2023. Red and yellow lanterns neatly decorated the town squares, signifying good fortune and letting go.

Then, there is the Dragon Boat Festival, which commemorates poet Qu Yuan. Before the Dragon Boat Festival in Penghu, we assembled a team of Fulbrighters and local college students to compete in a boat race. We practiced twice a week starting at the beginning of June to prepare for the race in Magong Harbor.

During June, I missed one week of practice because I traveled to Tainan to stay at Shangri-La's Far Eastern Plaza Hotel, Tainan to visit Chimei Museum, Qi Shiseido Salon and Spa, and some food hotspot recommendations that Pingtung Fulbrighter and Yale Graduate Harry Rubin gave me. But I returned, and on June 22, 2023, we competed in Magong Harbor against several teams.

We were recognized as the best international team to compete in the holiday race. A photo of Maggie Wu, Maiya Peterson, Malka Schnaidman, and I showed up in the national newspaper the same day in our life jackets, about to enter the boat. In the photo, I was two Taiwan Beers down on an empty stomach at 11 a.m. It was a fun day. Our coaches were from the local university—Shirle and Torulf Karlsson. Shirle, my Chinese teacher, brought me a competition shirt, a unique shell gift, and some brand-new Mandarin books to study. After the race, Torulf ordered some Prosecco to celebrate.

There is a holiday called Grappling with the Goat, held during Ghost Month in July. During this month, many believe ghosts haunt the island. This celebration is as close as one could get to an elongated Halloween. Then, there is the Mid-Autumn Festival, held after the first Autumn Harvest. On this date, people thank God and eat moon cakes. Moon cakes are supposed to represent the moon and the act of moon-watching during the festival. In America, the only thing close to this may be the Fourth of July—a day we launch artificial lights into the sky in the form of fireworks instead of worshiping the moon as they do in Taiwan. I received countless mung bean, taro, and pineapple mooncakes during the Mid-Autumn Festival.

Zhongyuan Festival, also known as Zhongyuan Pudu, is when all the locals prepare chicken, fish, and duck dishes to exchange. On this day, many families pray for their lost loved ones to have great salvation and an afterlife. The Aboriginal festival is an intimate local tribal celebration. Buddhist temples host the celebration for Guanin's Birthday (the goddess of mercy). The main places where the festival takes place are the Longshan Temple in Taipei (a beautiful spot I visited during my first eight days of quarantine in Taiwan) and the Zizhu Temple. Merry says there are martial arts performances and food distribution on this day.

The Yimin Festival happens every year in July to remember the Hakka militia group that fought during the 1700s. There is then Double Ninth Day. In Asian culture, the number nine symbolizes male energy or yang. To celebrate this meaning, the Taiwanese celebrate on September 9 every year. The activities include anything that may signify male vitality, such as hill climbing, walking, kite flying, and drinking wine.

Finally, the Mazu Birthday and Pilgrimage is considered one of the world's most significant religious events. I was intrigued by this event when hearing about it at my Fulbright orientation at Danshui Fisherman's Wharf in New Taipei. After watching a documentary filmed above the country of Taiwan, highlighting the many attractions of the country, I learned about the pilgrimage and what it means for religious locals. Devotees march toward the Dajia Temple with the Mazu Deity. This event, usually in March or April, is celebrated with a lot of food, dancing, and prayers to Mazu.

Wildly, according to Round Taiwan Round, there is a sea in Ruifang District, New Taipei City, called the Yin Yang Sea, where the water mixes yellow and blue due to concentrated ions in the water. It is highly recommended not to enter the water (roundTAIWANround 2015). Somewhat metaphorically, the name of this sea exemplifies the importance and potency of the symbol that has come to symbolize balance universally in the world. As well, there is a safer sea in Taiwan called Sun Moon Lake, located in the middle of Taiwan, known for bike riding, delicious food, and a large indigenous population, according to its government website (Sun Moon Lake National Scenic Area Administration 2019). Again, the name alludes to a beautiful balancing of two energies. The sun: male, dominant, yang. The moon: female, passive, yin. The fact that it is the name of one of the most well-known lakes in the world exemplifies its place within culture as a symbol representing so much more than simply a religion or belief system. The black and white sign and the many iterations of its meaning represent a way of life and a concept far beyond our imagination.

In a conversation on June 2, 2021, with Academy-Award-winning actor Matthew McConaughey, Sadhguru, author of *Karma: A Yogi's Guide to Crafting Destiny,* speaks about his wisdom as a practicing yogi and mystic. He states explicitly that within the world, there exist no contradictions but rather a beautiful mosaic of complements. This sentiment illuminates the meaning of yin and yang. Without one, the other would not exist and vice versa. The natural wave of one into the other and the smaller dots within each allow both energies to coexist in beautiful harmony (Sadhguru 2021).

Furthermore, our senses can perceive because of the specific context around us. Without context, our minds would not sense anything. We would be inherently lost as we live in a state of relationality and connectivity. In this way, many humans do not understand that the universe is cosmic, and everything builds on each other in a very karmic way. We must realize that we are all inherently connected and blessed to live life through an individualistic lens. While listening to Sadhguru, I took a break to talk with my students, who all vary in age.

Speaking to them efficiently and effectively was hyper-challenging, not only because of the language barrier but because of the difference in age and cultural background between us. In the same sense of darkness and light, our Western and Eastern cultures complement each other while allowing us to grow exponentially. The one item I searched for was our difference in world views and how we approach our lives.

Growing up studying history and the world, I learned that many paint Americans as selfish, while the Eastern way of life was far more altruistic and family oriented. While working in the classroom and getting dinner with several teachers weekly, I realized these seemingly separate worldviews were naturally related and intertwined. And as Sadhguru examines, they are entirely complementary. Naturally, one must take advantage of their point of view to serve the world. Sadhguru goes as far as to say that "being selfless" is impossible as it does not exist. He means that because we experience life from a specific point of view, it is impossible to be selfless as our particular vantage point is inherently different from every other. The key, however, is to ask yourself: "Is my selfishness inclusive or exclusive?" This methodical question pinpoints the purpose and approach of your inwardness and unique point of view.

I found that several of the locals and my co-teachers work to live and pay the bills. Because they are so focused on work, they rarely have time to have a fun life outside of work, meaning several of them live alone. I also discovered when chatting with Doctor Nadeau, the president of Fulbright Taiwan, that the child population of Taiwan is decreasing as people have stopped getting married and have chosen not to expand their families. Ironically, a couple of weeks after hearing about this trend, the world population reached eight billion people on

Wednesday, November 16, 2022, in the afternoon on Taiwan time. With no family to serve or commit to, the Confucian belief of serving a family is not as prominent in one's life. Therefore, a more selfish life is almost guaranteed. When delving into this label of "selfishness," I began to understand that this is, in fact, natural, and being "selfish" is essential for growth and service to others and the world. Self-confidence and security depend on selfishness. No matter what culture one is in, the more focused and controlled people will accomplish more, which requires a certain level of self-reflection and a self-serving nature.

I noticed that students who were more successful in the classroom also naturally had more confidence in their abilities and themselves. It was beautiful to see this care they had for themselves on full display, attempting to connect with me in the process and leading many of their classmates. What I thought would be a discrepancy or a difference in how we went about our lives was somewhat interconnected and similar. I laughed with my co-teachers and students, who loved making jokes and having fun with me. Even though I am American and naturally lived a life of looking forward to a hopeful future, it excited them, and they liked encouraging me and supporting me. My students always yelled my name, and my co-teacher Leo enjoyed calling me "Hercules."

I realized that simplifying interactions and thinking led to smoother communication and exchanges. Sadhguru expresses this phenomenon beautifully, explaining that our intelligence sometimes causes us to be so wrapped up in individuality. He explains, "Once you understand that everything is connected, you live through your humanity." As tai chi represents, energy connects the whole universe, and we as humans are merely floating in existence as the same. In his discussion, Sadhguru brings different opposites to the table, comparing being compulsive with being conscious and too committed to lifestyle rather than life. When we forgo this compulsive, animalistic behavior, we realize we are living creatures breathing like plants and bugs on the ground. Once we reconnect with nature and its beauty, we can open ourselves up to life's incredible simplicity and the beauty it truly has to offer. Once we understand that life is not about achievements and constant comparison but simply about enjoyment and fulfilling our purpose, we can flow more efficiently while connecting with nature on a higher level.

As we sipped on the local tea of Penghu, Principal Bruce gave me an exciting peek inside his family life. Interestingly, he exclaimed that he does not want his kids to go to his school while explaining that he usually lets his wife make essential decisions.

He discussed that our curriculum was not centered around strictly studying because a child's life should be holistic and filled with fun experiences. He also pointed out that the fault in many families worldwide and several in Asia is their stress on IQ. He then pointed out, "There are three other measures to stress just as much, if not more."

Three include AQ, EQ, and MQ or Adversity Quotient, Emotional Quotient, and Moral Quotient. Bruce continued, "For a child to develop into the best version of themselves, they need to develop all four cornerstones together fully."

I agree. Intelligence is not the end-all be-all. It is one piece of a pie constantly evolving and changing depending on your circumstances. I found it incredibly heart-warming that my principal's sentiments matched my thoughts while directly contrasting several principals' belief that in today's world overworking students is the answer to creating world leaders who can change our planet. In reality, building a well-rounded human being is the only way to create a better future for our world where people can be themselves freely without having to change who they are, be constantly stressed, or worry uncontrollably about a lot that will never be known.

Sitting in a hut by the ocean, nearing Thanksgiving—an American holiday expressing gratitude for those in your life—I was tranquil and at complete peace. I realized I am just stardust on a planet, constantly learning and growing. Being my best is all I can do. In all its wonder and fish, Taiwan and my home in Penghu helped me recognize this and awaken my senses.

Aimen Beach

Arcade Downtown with Milksha Drink

Beichen Market

Boat ride around archipelago

Boat Ride continued

Chiang Kai-Shek Memorial Hall in Taipei

Favorite gelato place in Penghu

Field Trip to nearby island with students

Best Hot Pot in Magong County

Field trip to Dongji and Dongyuping

Dream Beach

Eating a lot of noodles in Downtown Magong

Teaching How to Set a Table

Yuwei Chang, Myself, and Deborah Broomer

First day of school with Principal Bruce

Oyster Omelet

Fishing

Lizhengjiao Beach

Opening New Turf Soccer Field with Former Magistrate of Penghu County, Lai Feng-wei

Popular Night Market in Taipei

Teaching eighth and ninth grade English with Teacher Leo

Teaching water sports

Popular temple in Xiyu Township

The Eatery

PART 2:

DOUBLE-SIDED SOCIETY

Live Life like a Sponge Rather than a Sprinkler, but Also like a Stone

———

"We are very very small. But we are profoundly capable of very very big things."
—STEPHEN HAWKING

I sauntered into a charming tea house called Wang An Cafe behind my incomparable co-teachers, Mr. Tsai and Mr. Leo. Our entourage featured a tall, slender white man and two popular local teachers born and raised in Asia. As I walked in, I took in the unusual surroundings: the candle-infused smell, the bright crosses on the wall, the three overweight cats roaming the floors like ghosts, the modern bar to the left with wine and liquor lining the lit-up, mirrored shelves behind.

My co-teachers had fun personalities. One was a few ciga-
rettes and drinks into the night already, and the other acted
like my twin—a giddy, adventurous, young-at-heart soul. I
have grown to love them despite my Mandarin language
deficiencies. We came from dinner at one of the finest seafood restaurants in downtown Magong City for a nightcap
and to discuss the future.

"I will miss you both when this is all over," I said, honest
and sharp.

"Are you going back to America in July of 2023," they both
responded as if rehearsed. I could see the boundless wonder
in their eyes. I felt like their child in many ways.

"Yes, I am. I want to make the most of all the time we have
left." I leaned down to grab the menu. I ordered a Kahlua
cocktail and ask what they want. As I age, I realize time is as
fleeting as the short buzz of my cocktails. Each moment falls
into the next uncontrollably and faster with each passing year.

We spent the next hour laughing and chatting about boxing,
Taiwanese news, world religions, pets, and lifestyles. The
more I learned about them and Taiwanese culture, the happier I became. The more information available to me, the
more I grasped it. I was a sponge.

When I think of a quintessential sponge ready to take on any
adventure, I think of a famous animated sponge. I picture
SpongeBob SquarePants, a cartoon sponge who lives in a
pineapple under the sea in his self-titled hit cartoon show
called *SpongeBob SquarePants*. SpongeBob, the protagonist

of his story, is energetic and always ready to learn, grow, and go on an adventure. His life is one big journey of self-discovery and enjoyment. His many famous phrases epitomize positivity and awe, starting from the first episode of a show that has run for over twenty years and is still running today (Drymon and Hillenburg 1999).

A sponge soaks up water as if it depends on it for survival—constantly curious to learn and grow. A leader or any person full of wisdom must lead like a sponge.

Forbes published an article by the Forbes Leadership Forum on July 5, 2012, detailing the apparent misconception surrounding the most successful CEOs in the world that pure intellectuality got them to where they are rather than intellectual curiosity. Of course, they are brilliant, but what makes them stand out is their inquisitive nature and insatiable desire to learn and grow. This mind-set entails listening to peers and mentors, developing relationships or studying from those who came before, and consuming information via written work (Forbes Leadership Forum 2012).

However, the balance between being a consumer and delivering is vitally important. One must be able to use that information creatively or in a way that can help them reach their desired destination. The *Forbes* article (2012) describes this physically, using the word "stone." A "stone" is fearless, multi-dimensional, and unafraid to peer down multiple avenues to prove themselves wrong. When one door closes, another one will inevitably open. Stones are aware of this and take advantage of it. I know many stones who never accept "no" for an answer.

A thick rather than fine line exists between being a "sponge" and a "stone." The balance of learning and acting, rather than simply acting all the time—demanding what others should do or being ungrateful for what is already in front of you—is essential to understand. That is why being both expressive and receptive is so important to connect deeper with others and be more successful in everyday encounters. A strategic stone does not throw itself at every opportunity uncontrollably, and an intelligent sponge does not soak up too much information to the point of overload. The pair works together powerfully as a balanced yin (sponge) and yang (stone) combination, returning to level ground in times of imbalance.

As previously referenced, a famous character that also happens to be a sponge is SpongeBob from the animated show *SpongeBob SquarePants*, which began in 1999 and continues to this day. This animated comedy show has been wildly popular, and the character SpongeBob stands for much goodness in the modern world. Like a sponge in real life, SpongeBob lives a half-full life, excited to explore with his best friend, Patrick. Like SpongeBob, we should make the most out of what we are given. For him, it was jelly fishing, working at The Krusty Krab, and trying to get his boat-driving license. He was filled with wild engagement and starry eyes in all his adventures, excited to take on any challenge. This personality epitomizes what a sponge represents: open, nonjudgmental, and exhilarated to try new activities (Drymon and Hillenburg 1999).

A spectrum of action and inaction carries the yin-yang symbol. However, for it to run smoothly, life needs to be running smoothly: optimistic and purpose filled. Being both a great listener and a humble actor in life enables you to manifest your goals and dreams that you want to achieve more efficiently. Introvert or extravert, feeler or thinker, outdoorsy or indoorsy, intently listening takes effort and skill. A person with a more yin-heavy personality may be better suited for listening. Still, a yang person may be just as good. They may need to adapt their vibration a little for accommodation.

WHY LISTENING LIKE A SPONGE MATTERS

I was at a bar called Freud Bistro in Magong City, watching the 2022 Soccer World Cup. I went with some local teachers, who were both from the United States. I had met several Caucasian teachers from England, Ireland, and North America who had been teaching in Taiwan for years through a football group I am part of, started by local teacher Larry Davis. While sitting in Freud, people-watching in one of the most popular bars in Penghu, I realized many people do not even try to listen.

Being a sponge means being willing to listen rather than dominating a conversation or thinking that simply presence is enough in any given situation as opposed to genuine attention. According to licensed marriage and family therapist Michelle C. Brooten-Brooks, in her Verywell Health article published on April 27, 2022, verbal connections are how we survive because it is one of our brain's dire needs.

However, Brooten-Brooks explains that excessive talking is a problem and can even be linked to certain mental disorders such as bipolar, schizophrenia, personality disorders, anxiety, and ADHD. I have seen it within my family and friends who suffer from these conditions. Sometimes, especially during manic episodes, I have had to listen to angry rants or disorganized-out-loud thinking. Talking too much is usually not a good sign. There are four categories of excessive talking:

- Pressured speech is urgent and allows no one to get a word in. Several students in my classes growing up represented this population: overconfident and overbearing, dominating the conversation and leaving a bad taste in several other students' mouths.
- Hyperverbal speech, common when meeting new people, is fast speech with a high heart rate. Some Taiwanese I talked to in the fall had this when I first met them.
- Disorganized speech is rapid speech that does not follow a linear path.
- Compulsive talking, mirroring the actions of many people performing compulsive behavior, is uncontrollable and often forgoes allowing anyone else to get a word in edgewise in a conversation (Brooten-Brooks 2022)

The key is being a sponge and avoiding this brash "yang" behavior, so slow down, stop talking, and listen with presence and a nuanced restraint. Timers may be a beautiful tool to treat conversations with opportunity cost, realizing that every interaction is happening when another one could be happening. Try to notice details and social cues in every interaction rather than viewing a conversation as an annoying obligation about you and for you.

While in Freud with my bright blue famous "Absolute Drunk" drink in my hands, I realized several people in the room were not listening to any words from those around them at their table. Many would not even look into the eyes of the other person. It seemed as though several people were not enjoying the food in front of them or taking the time to soak in the scenery of the bar. I realized it is not uncommon for people to become numb to their surroundings, losing their gratitude and lust for life because they lack the fortitude to insert themselves at the moment to enjoy the people and the places in front of them.

Being a sponge may be different or complex, depending on your personality type. Introverts versus extroverts may have a better time listening. Still, extroverts may have less difficulty keeping conversations alive enough to expose important information. This spectrum of openness is fascinating to dive deeper into to understand that yin and yang may have specific homes during these periods of reclusion and exposure. Naturally, a great sponge can listen like no one else but also has the flamboyance to place itself in critical situations that manifest magical moments.

WHAT LISTENING ACTUALLY IS

Furthermore, listening is often misclassified. Listening does not mean consuming passively. According to a 2016 Harvard Business Review article titled "What Great Listeners Actually Do" by Jack Zenger and Joseph Folkman, listening involves actively probing for information through questions, challenging the person they speak to. Also, listeners build up the speaker positively by verbally supporting them with confidence. A cooperative conversation does not involve defensive communication but rather involves a two-way feedback system that is welcomed by both and feels balanced. Listening is not nodding and memorizing silently. A sponge can soak up much more interesting information in an environment conducive to that happening: balanced and encouraging. So while lending an ear is fantastic, the ear means nothing if the initiative to further the conversation and raise the vibration is not there. This initiative is the "stone" (Zenger and Folkman 2016).

In my eyes, I see it like receiving and giving—a dance, if you will. Whereas yin is the calm, composed listener, yang is the active prober, always ready to ask inquisitive questions. Both are needed to be the best counterpart in any conversation. The worst-case scenario would be annoying and oblivious overtalker or the sprinkler, who fails to realize that they are spouting too much and only ruining their chances of personal growth, balance, and likability within a group.

I think an immature stone becomes a sprinkler, spraying unwanted droplets everywhere. A mature human being exhibiting a growth mind-set will understand that a "sprinkler" is not the proper way to express oneself as it is messy, overbearing, and often too much. A sponge acts with empathy while a sprinkler acts with an attitude highly focused on personal gain most of the time.

When the sponge and stone, yin and yang, come together, they create a composed and active listener and, therefore, a strong leader ready to make substantial changes. You cannot act appropriately without understanding correctly. And you cannot understand properly without listening properly. Yang meets yin, and expression follows the reception.

THE UNSTOPPABLE MINDFUL SPONGE AND STONE COMBO

It was Monday, November 28, 2022. The end of 2022 was fast approaching, like the headlights on a speeding car in the distance. My friend Tommy Nguyen, a Vietnam Fulbrighter and fellow USC Graduate, and Warren Bennis Scholar visited Taiwan and Penghu for a few days until December 1. Throughout the week, while discussing the differences between Asian countries and North America, along with exploring Pier 3 Mall, bar-hopping into Freud Bistro, and enjoying snowflake ice cream at 23.5° Cactus Ice Cream, I took him to Long Xing Restaurant and Addict Restaurant with a few of my buddies in downtown Magong, two of the best restaurants in the city.

From Long Xing, we enjoyed the usual family-style dinner (squid with mayo, pumpkin noodles, tuna sashimi, prawns, grilled grouper, grilled oyster teriyaki, conch, and peanut puffs) in a private room downstairs. We guzzled a few bottles of Classic Taiwan Beer, winter melon tea, and green tea to wash down all the food with many laughs. At Addict Restaurant, we each ordered the Chef's Spread, which featured pumpkin soup, seafood salad, a main course, sweet potato churros, and a drink—gin and kombucha for me.

I asked each of them what mindfulness meant to them.

My friend Gerardy Jean-Philippe II, a 2023 Charles B. Rangel International Affairs Graduate Fellow in Taiwan to teach for his fourth year, responded with the ability to live in the moment and to truly appreciate each second for what it is. My roommate Gabo Chaffee, a Rodriguez Scholar from Olin Business School at Washington University in St. Louis, decided it was taking time to observe and recognize the unique and nonreplicable experiences around you. Tommy looked up from his yellow pumpkin soup and baguette, simply replying, "Making the most of every situation." Within all definitions, I saw a requirement or a common denominator: intentional action through deep care in what you do—in other words, putting yourself in a mental state to enjoy what is in front of you.

I agree with my friends, but there is another layer to observing and taking full advantage of every situation. For any observation to be perceived correctly, there must be a switch in yourself: using your soul, not your ego. Kute Blackson, in his book, *The Magic of Surrender: Finding the Courage to Let Go*, explains this phenomenon: "Soul lives in total honesty and integrity… Soul tunes in to what the body needs, knowing there is nothing to prove" (Blackson 2022). Whereas ego locks us in a cage of righteousness and a small self-absorbed bubble of continuous effort, living with our soul unlocks unlimited potential as we surrender to life's many teachings that it can offer in every little moment.

Developing this surrendering mindfulness may be challenging, especially for those dedicated to a specific structure and rigid plan their whole lives. Even my friends here in Penghu have difficulty surrendering, and I do not blame them. It can be challenging to let your soul shine in a new atmosphere with new people around you. But this surrendering may enable you to find a balance between your internal sponge and stone and yin and yang.

The next day, I woke up at 5 a.m., my usual time. I prepared for my discussion with Alexandra Keller, a woman committed to raising collective consciousness in the United States through psychedelic integration, reiki practice, and mindfulness meditation. I was hunkered down in my apartment in Penghu, Taiwan, fresh from a coffee trip to 7-Eleven in the haze of a post-rainy night. I downed two Mr. Brown coffees, enjoying every last sip. I opened my laptop to Keller in the basement of her home in Pennsylvania. Going into the interview, I felt mindful and attentive. Usually, caffeine allowed me to focus and prepare well for interviews, enabling me to think faster, listen better, and follow up correctly. I related to Keller, and I wanted her to be receptive to my genuine interest.

"When I healed myself, I wanted to heal others." Keller dealt with trauma growing up and finally was able to put it behind her after developing mindfulness mechanisms to reach deeper into her subconscious to become who she was always meant to become—her authentic self.

When I asked about her clients and their motives, she revealed that most came to her for "consciousness expansion." In other words, they wanted to live on a plateau where their most authentic and highest form of self could shine through—a state of being where the past and the future did not exist. The journey might be arduous, but the goal remained the same— reaching a state where "just being" becomes normalized to the point where there is nothing to prove, and there is no need to be anxious, worried, or hurried.

Being a sponge in this state is easy. It is natural because all one has to do is give themselves full attention, time, and care to achieve their desires. Sometimes patience, humility, and direction are the best answers to fall into this serene river of peace, prosperity, and consistency—a free-flowing river where learning is a way of life and being present is second nature. Afterward, the toggle from sponge state to stone state can take place. In other words, meditate to empty your mind so a breakthrough thought can come into your mind, and then you can take action.

Exploring this idea deeper with Keller, we found that inherently what is within us creates what is outside us. Keller declared, "What we experience in our outer world is a direct reflection of what is going on in our inner world."

When we develop an awareness of our consciousness, we become aware of who we are and get to know this living "collective consciousness" that binds us together in our shared human experience. A sponge can recognize this invisible connection that inherently binds us all together as human beings, almost succumbing to the Buddhist belief of "impermanence" and the Christian idea of denying oneself.

As part of this conscious collective, we grow when we can grow the collective as well. This intelligent recognition, knowing a "collective consciousness" and even a "divine consciousness" exists allows us to understand that we are part of something bigger, operating on a higher frequency of existence.

Without each other, we would never understand anything. A sponge recognizes the power in the collective and in genuinely immersing oneself in different cultures and moments. Nothing should be deemed unworthy of exploration. Because it exists, it is worthy of that existence as it is part of our shared collective.

As both a sponge and a stone, we can cultivate inner peace like SpongeBob by being curious, asking essential questions, and taking the initiative to enter rooms we would like to be in. A sponge is always utilizing situations to their benefit, trying to make sense of every moment and understanding their place within the moment. A stone is taking proactive steps, using newfound information positively and innovatively. Once again, it is about developing balance because a symmetrical dynamic of both sponge (yin) and stone (yang) is a gentle, powerful, and present force; take your time to develop yourself and do not overly rush yourself into a situation, forcing what time has planned for you. Be a sponge. Be a stone. Just keep soaking. Just keep stepping.

CHAPTER 9

Through Suffering, Life Matters Exponentially

―――

"We are healed of a suffering only by experiencing it to the full."
—MARCEL PROUST, *IN SEARCH OF LOST TIME*

I sometimes struggle with relationships. Not because I want to. I desire great relationships, but it is challenging to maintain consistency when moving around and growing as a person. When I commit to a relationship, I sometimes over-deliver and end up disappointed with the return. I sometimes defer to the side of being less hands-on for the sake of protecting my effort, emotions, and time.

The relationship ends with suffering for the other person or me, juggling how much time and effort should be put into this dynamic, especially if it is a temporary connection. But through suffering and working through deep struggles, I have found my most robust companions in the world—bonds that are lifelong and extremely permanent, like a tattoo on the soul. Despite well-intentions, much suffering comes about through relationships and navigating deep feelings and desires.

A pair of people working well together is often challenging and rarely straightforward. Within the intricacies of the couple's development, there is bound to be disappointment, pain, fighting, and disagreement. But there is also love, learning, growth, and much fun. Relationships epitomize the reward of working through difficult times because the more valleys a relationship goes through, the stronger it may become.

The teacher and student pairing in my life has been around for a while, since I was five years old, to be exact. I have had both great teachers and horrible teachers. The great teachers were usually animated, caring, and flexible while the horrendous teachers were boring, bland, or lacking relatability. The dynamic between my students and me as a teacher was painful because I came to Penghu without any knowledge of the local language—Mandarin with some Taiwanese flavor here and there.

This challenge was an immediate struggle because I could not be funny or laugh with them naturally. August, September, and October were filled with trial and error. I used the three main tactics of repeating myself, testing the waters of comprehension, and observing body language to gauge how, exactly, I could relate to seventh, eighth, and ninth graders from an island off the coast of an island in the Asia Pacific.

Despite being a hump I had to overcome—or instead, because it was a hump I had to overcome—the other side was much more beautiful and worthwhile. The challenge made the reward and the process much more satisfying, gratifying, and wholeheartedly worth it.

I often read in self-help books growing up and in religious works such as the Bible that fighting for something or working toward a goal will often cause a countercurrent of persecution, hate, or doubt from people around you who oppose your beliefs or do not like you. This opposition is significant because life is not supposed to be easy, and pushing through these clouds is hyper-necessary to reach a more substantial, solid ground of confidence, conciseness, and clarity.

Yongey Mingyur Rinpoche—a Tibetan Buddhist teacher, best-setting author, and leader of the Tergar Meditation Community—explains the concept of pain in "Getting to Know Suffering." In Sanskrit, "suffering" is a translation of "duhkha," which means "non-satisfaction" (Rinpoche 2014). This absent feeling, unfortunately, familiar in the sometimes-greedy United States population today, is present with a lack of appreciation and gratitude for what is sitting right in front of you. Americans often feel as if they are incomplete and missing some piece, which translates to suffering and pain. Often, we think about suffering as a reaction to external stimuli such as getting hurt or a series of unfortunate circumstances.

However, suffering is a mental state within
us, causing us to feel imperfect, lacking,
and insufficient.

According to Yongey Rinpoche, the first teaching of the Buddha was after he achieved enlightenment in India under the famous Bodhi tree in the central part of India called Bodhgaya. After this, the Buddha went to Varanasi to give the first-ever dharma talk. The first teaching had five students. And his first sentiment was, "Life is suffering." This teaching aimed to help learn and understand the "nature of suffering" to liberate yourself from it by separating yourself from the physical suffering (Rinpoche 2014).

Buddha famously expressed his view in the Four Noble Truths that suffering is synonymous with the human condition but so is the end of suffering through awakening. Just as you do to eliminate a disease, you must reflect, examine, and analyze yourself to view your suffering from a bird's-eye view. Radically accept your grief, and then you can separate yourself and consider it for what it is. Essentially, suffering is necessary, undoubtedly present, and even beneficial. It molds and configures us deeply, allowing us to discover ourselves and grow intrinsically from within.

Pain and pleasure are diametrically opposite. Suppose you asked one what they would prefer for a day. In that case, there is no doubt that they would most likely gravitate toward pleasure—a day of pleasurable behavior without any hiccups, bumps, or bruises. This lifestyle may sound beautiful, but it is not only hedonistic but utterly contrary to what one needs for growth, maturation, and discovery.

According to a creatively produced May 2019 TEDEd video called "The Mysterious Science of Pain" by Joshua W. Pate, pain and tissue damage do not always equal. In other words, our minds can cause us to experience pain disproportionate to the actual injury. That is because this intricate puzzle has two pieces: "the experience of pain and the biological process called nociception" (Pate 2019).

Your body wants to protect you, and the sensors in your nerve endings detect threats and send signals to your brain. Then, the brain acknowledges these signals to weigh their validity before producing a feeling of "pain" to say you need protection. However, people who experience prolonged or chronic pain may have more sensitive receptors that unleash pain easier (Pate 2019).

How we experience pain and ultimately suffer has to do with our environment. This phenomenon is why therapy has become a hot topic in today's culture; physical therapists, clinical psychologists, nurses, and pain specialists work together to help heal. Turning off specific brain circuits in the amygdala, the middle region of the brain that involves fight or flight processing, can sometimes decrease pain (Pate 2019).

All this to say, pain and suffering are primarily predicated on brain functioning, which changes due to your day-to-day environment. Life is not about avoiding pain but accepting it and embracing it when blossoming into someone who has weathered the storm. People grow numb to the effect of activities that they always do. Do you want to get used to pain or pleasure? You choose. I would instead save pleasure after a hard week as a beautiful reward or for a celebration of hard work. I'd take the pain any day. The pain makes regular life all the sweeter.

Pain in school, for example, can come from academic pressure, social anxiety, or bullying from teachers and classmates. A school atmosphere can be dangerous and is often a place that pushes young men or women to grow up and find themselves. As a teacher and a learner throughout my life, I have witnessed pain in my students and classmates from failing or not connecting fully with a teacher or the subject matter. This pain from school can be dramatized, but it can often be the catalyst that turns a student into a diamond.

In the hard-hitting and beautiful book, *Supernormal: The Untold Story of Adversity and Resilience,* Author Meg Jay, PhD, describes children who grow up to become "supernormal" or extraordinarily resilient due to their overwhelming circumstances and past trauma. The hostility or unpredictability of their environment—whether due to siblings, supervisors, teachers, or parents—causes these high-performing children to have an enlarged amygdala. This enlarged amygdala translates to higher alertness, heightened arousal in potentially dangerous situations, and greater sensitivity to surroundings. These children develop these qualities through an unrelenting "fight or flight" mechanism, enhancing their heroic coping strategies for life's obstacles (Jay 2017).

Sometimes, the best students are students who have been through more demanding tests than they are taking now.

A scantron is no match for withstanding abuse or learning to maintain a sense of normalcy in real life. Frequently, understanding real-life scenarios help students understand the worlds of history, literature, and even art. Also, real-life struggles increase stamina and mental fortitude in any examination in the classroom or on the court.

PAIN ENABLES COMFORT

In the Holy Bible, 2 Corinthians 1: 5–6 reads, "For just as we share abundantly in the sufferings of Christ, so also our comfort abounds through Christ. If we are distressed, it is for your comfort and salvation; if we are comforted, it is for your comfort, which produces in you patient endurance of the same sufferings we suffer."

Suffering allows us to feel comfortable.

Without suffering, there would be no pleasurable sense available to us. A natural connective wave must occur to fully experience both ends of the pendulum. We should not get addicted to either end, but one end makes the other more important, vivid, and potent in our lives. Just as the beautiful sunrise brightens the dark deepness of the night, pleasure is exponential through pain. The white dot on the yang side of the yin yang and the black dot on the yin side of the yin yang—each side must have a component of the other to be in balance. Like this combination, suffering also has an element of comfort, as in the Corinthians quote, and comfort has an aspect of suffering.

Coming out through a tunnel or a traumatic situation enables the light at the end to be refreshing, fulfilling, and empowering. Do not be afraid to live, love, and laugh. Through heartbreak and experiences, we build a foundation of who we are and who we are supposed to become. Although life can and will be painful, it is always worth it, no matter what. You come out of it with an epic story or a lesson learned.

Coming to Taiwan, I had to adjust majorly to simplifying my language for students to grasp. No longer could I use long words or try explaining every detail. I had to restructure and reframe the way I had taught before to use actions rather than words. Through suffering to teach, I became a better teacher. Either way, growth is always working in your favor when you try. Smile about it. The biggest lesson I learned while teaching was that presence is nearly everything, and if one can be genuinely engaged, encouraging, and optimistic in the classroom atmosphere, learning will primarily be an uplifting and successful experience.

I am an avid massage goer and fanatic. Massages reconnect your body, mind, and soul beautifully. Through deep tissue involvement, your nerves, muscles, and joints are pressured beautifully, allowing your body to release tension and reclaim a sense of tranquility. Massages are like therapy—sometimes painful but always leaving me wanting more. My body feels a sense of pure healing and extreme satisfaction.

Interestingly, the more pain I go through during a massage, the better I feel afterward. The agony of some of the pressure points is always worth it when you stand up and feel the prior unevenness slowly disappear.

According to Emory University's chair of the Department of Psychiatry and Behavioral Sciences, Mark Hyman Rapaport, frequent massages decrease the number of stress hormones, vasopressin, and cortisol in the body. According to their studies, which involved a control group, a group with one weekly massage, and a group with two weekly massages, a massage a week profoundly affected the immune system, and a massage twice a week increased oxytocin (Rapaport 2012).

This work, published on YouTube on September 17, 2012, was funded by the National Center for Complementary and Alternative Medicine. Of course, diet, exercise, and nutrition may help as well as conventional pharmacotherapy. No matter what the care is, some sense of pain or hard work must always go into the healing process. Ultimately, as Emory's in-depth studies show, the more frequent the massages are, the better mood one is in due to lowered levels of stress and higher levels of oxytocin (Rapaport 2012).

Saturday, November 19, 2022 I was back in the capital city of Taiwan, Taipei, for the Fulbright Thanksgiving Dinner conference. I flew in the day before and stayed at Green World Hotel Zhonghua. The beautiful conference happened at the Great Skyview Hotel in the afternoon, where I met award-winning artist Yosifu Kacaw and his brilliant portrayal of specific emotions through primary colors—depictions of true beauty within struggle.

On Sunday, a day after the Fulbright conference, called Vitality of Taiwanese Indigenous Art and Culture, I visited a local massage parlor for a great deal of a thirty-minute foot and thirty-minute full body massage in Da'an District, Taipei.

After speaking with the owner about his journey and watching some Taiwanese karaoke on the television, I enjoyed a new employee's deep tissue massage on both my feet and back. Although very painful at some moments, even causing me to curl my toes due to the pain, the massage was very well done and left me in a state of relaxation and a bubble of Zen. I realized this massage was much more worthwhile than one I received at a local massage shop in downtown Magong City, Penghu because it was more painful and deep.

LET'S BE REAL: MOST OF OUR SUFFERING IS STRESS

From personal experience, I know stress can ruin days, weeks, or even months of someone's life. Out of everything in life, stress has almost always been the number one trigger for unhappiness or mental health issues. Where I am from, just south of Palo Alto, where Stanford University is located, I would hear about several suicides every year due to the stress students face from the pressure of their future weighing over their heads. Whenever I finished my final exams each year, I felt as if I had just completed a full mental marathon and could finally exhale.

Stress has changed meaning and shape-shifted over the years due to discoveries. According to the brilliant 2019 documentary, *Stressed* by Director Luke Segreto, if we can harness our stress and relinquish the control it has over our body, we can reach into our true essence and change the course of human history one by one. Stress arose naturally when hunter-gatherers in 70000 BCE had to survive predators with pure instinct.

According to this film by Segreto and presented by the ONE Research Foundation, the study of stress began in 1637 when René Descartes coined the famous phrase, "I think, therefore I am" (ONE Research Foundation 2020). Descartes was referring to mind-body dualism, in which the body cannot exist without the mind because it is the only thinking piece in the whole body. In 1854, Claude Bernard acknowledged that the internal environment within a human must remain constant in response to a change in the external environment. This phenomenon is what Walter Bradford Cannon labeled "homeostasis" in 1936. Stress is not worrying; it is all your body's responses to stimuli, desiring to keep your body stable. The problem is that stress can cause unnecessary weight to be placed on you. Christine Cohn exclaims:

> Stress causes almost every condition out there. If we can just take some of that emotional pressure off their system, at least the chemistry of that emotion, their body has a better chance to heal (ONE Research Foundation 2020).

Stress comes directly from our autonomic nervous system utilizing a "fight or flight" response, contrary to the parasympathetic nervous system, which allows us to heal. Believe it or not, emotions are a physiological phenomenon rather than a mental construct. Emotions are run by neuropeptides connecting to receptors throughout the body (ONE Research Foundation 2020).

In the documentary, Jerry Lee, Doctor of Chiropractic, LAc, explains that "meridians" are channels throughout the body, allowing this free flow. Whenever a blockage occurs in the passageway, there is a disruption of "chi." Chi promoted by tai chi is the powerful force that connects our mind, body, and soul when effectively used at peace (ONE Research Foundation 2020).

The documentary focuses on the beautiful life that exists when the trauma that causes too much stress is healed. This healing can be done through the Neuro Emotional Technique (NET), where the physical and mental spaces are treated as emotional needs are often never rational. Through this innovative therapy, people can stabilize their bodies by stabilizing their emotions and vice versa as they flow into one another. The point is to neutralize past traumatic events to become more comfortable in your skin (ONE Research Foundation 2020).

Once this comfort is achieved, life is beautiful. We must understand that life is rocky, and emotions are rarely rational. Self-care allows the body to heal itself and become stronger than before. The pain is worth it because it molds us into the people we are today: more balanced, focused, and authentic to who we are and what we have to offer the world.

CHAPTER 10

Nature, Nurture, Nada

———

*"Everything that happens to us is the result of what we our-
selves have thought, said, or done. We alone are responsible
for our lives."*
—GAUTAMA BUDDHA

At the University of Southern California, I had the pleasure
of learning in a leadership cohort of people from all walks
of life and backgrounds, carrying on the legacy of Warren
Bennis, one of the world's leading authors and consultants. I
connected with Warren Bennis's work because of his strong
interest in human behavior and understanding people when
leading. I believe the importance of empathy and attitude
when forging success weaved through all of his work.

Through the program, I met philanthropist David C. Bohnett,
Doctor Ginny Baro, and many other successful and renowned
people in their respective fields. When asking them questions,
I understood that their lives were determined not by their
bones but by what the world had in store for them. Many

become who they are destined to be through effort, exploration, and karma.

Learning in the experiential learning center, a high-technol-
ogy state-of-the-art facility in the basement of the historic
Marshall School of Business, I have gleaned the importance
of every moment and the energy emitted. From case studies
on attitude to debriefs on how to build teams best, I have
come to a familiar conclusion. Life is often determined by
relationships, attitude, and the energy you emit rather than
the skills you have or how you were brought up.

Within this intensive two-year program, I took part in camps
and orientations. I studied The Art of Leadership—Self Discovery, The Art of Leadership—Leading on a Global Stage,
The Art of Leadership—Change Leadership, and The Art of
Leadership—Practical Leadership with USC Chief Enroll-
ment Officer Katharine Harrington, Political Activist Steven
Lamy, Entrepreneur Adlai Wertman, and Dean Varun Soni,
respectively, all of whom I call my dear friends, confidants,
and colleagues.

I grew up in a scientific household. My parents both studied
biological sciences at Stanford University. Because of this,
I was attuned to science: DNA, health, the natural world,
plants, cells, sickness, and medicine. I was also aware of the
debate between nature and nurture from a young age. My
parents were in the pharmaceutical business, so it was natural for me to be interested in nurture and how medicine
and supplements I can take can further my performance in
sports and school. I was interested in the bodily effects of

drinking caffeine, consuming creatine, reading books, and exercising often.

I was also interested in DNA and the connective tissue that binds humans together. Essentially, we are all stardust. As a kid, that thrilled me. This fact gave me a reason to believe that we all are the same and are simply humans roaming the planet as one.

When it comes down to this or that, my brain enjoys returning to the fact that we are all part of the same cosmos, floating in space and time. When I think of how insignificant I truly am, I feel weightless and less stressed out. Rather than focusing on nature or nurture, let us concentrate on nourishment: finding what fulfills us and pushing toward that daily to figure out who we are.

Nature versus nurture is a battle we often play out on discussion boards, in debate rooms, and within large teams. This tug of war match gets us nowhere fast. The truth is that neither is correct. Some hodgepodge combination of both creates who we are today.

The duality of these two concepts creates a shared portrait of who we are, what we express to the world, and what we will ultimately achieve in our lives. In their 2022 article, "The Nature vs. Nurture Debate," Psychologist Kendra Cherry and Doctor David Susman explain that the nature versus nurture debate arises in many contexts—from academic success and psychology to child development, personality development, and mental illness development.

Interestingly, the article explains that many researchers do not view nature and nurture against each other but rather see it as "nature with nurture." For example, recognizing music comes from a single gene, but being able to follow through with processing the music takes musical lessons when you are young. Height is another excellent example of the two working together well because genes for tallness only manifest themselves through proper nourishment during childhood development. Similar to life expectancy, height is a combination of biology and lifestyle (Cherry 2022).

The debate is never-ending because one will never trump the other in reality. The winner does not exist, unfortunately. Both sides of the spectrum are complementary and come together to depict the whole picture. Opportunity and options make up a lot of how our life turns out. By grinding out our life, we can create our traits. The problem is never the problem but rather our attitude toward that problem.

It is interesting to think about "mind" and "body." When speaking to Stanford graduate Yogi Theo Mann, who worked on Human Values in Design with IDEO founder David Kelley before lecturing about mind-set and creative problem-solving at Stanford, I realized that because stress is such a vocal point in determining our lives, so much of ourselves depends on how we train our minds in life. Bad times are inevitable, but how we bounce back determines how the rest of our lives play out, no matter what our biology has written in the stars for us.

Mann and I discussed this nurturing aspect that genuinely allows one's nature, or nurture, to shine. I believe great nature itself can never reap success. However, great nurture without unique nature can reap benefits. Mann discussed his thoughts on Ramana Maharshi, an Indian Hindu sage and jivanmukta. When he was still alive, many people discovered him meditating in the back of a temple, being bitten by bugs and rats. He continued meditating here peacefully because it was the only place young men would not bother him. Somehow, he could sit in a state of inner peace despite what was happening. Mann finds that genuinely inspirational. Maharshi's poise illustrates that no matter what is happening physically, we can accept our circumstances while making the most of them. Mann believes one has to practice feeling good in the mind to convince the body it is okay.

In this way, when delving deeper into spirituality and mindfulness, it is clearer to see that while yin and yang can be represented in the complementary force of nature and nurture, our ability to stabilize our mind through our nurturing may be the most crucial component to allowing these two forces to come together harmoniously. Without a stable mind with stable emotions to support our well-being, our skills and positive traits may be dimmed where nature cannot be fully realized.

I was born with a substantial gene base of parents who both graduated from Stanford University, played sports growing up, and challenged themselves physically, mentally, and socially. This luck meant that my biology would be pretty good, given this combination. However, my undying curiosity and determination have allowed me to earn a Fulbright scholarship and a degree from USC. The work ethic I developed as a young child to continuously strive to be my very best while stretching myself in any activity I participated in catapulted me further than my God-given skills or traits.

When I was younger, I developed a strong interest in magic. Learning card tricks takes time, focus, attention to detail, and practice. I remember specifically during the summer after my seventh-grade school year, I mastered sixteen individual card tricks and performed them for several people. One of these people was my grandpa, Pops. I taught him every single trick, going through each step one by one as he wrote them down.

I then watched him perform them for me, correcting and teaching him how to do each trick correctly. This card-teaching activity is just one of several instances where my interest drove my action and peaked my performance. Our attitude and follow-through on the subject matter or activity at hand dictate several outcomes in life. To be successful in any domain, you have to commit wholeheartedly to it while also developing a mind-set that promotes success and learning from failure.

One of my all-time favorite books I often keep on hand with me everywhere I venture, including Taiwan, is *Mindset: The New Psychology of Success* (2016). This book is a self-help book on the power of the mind to shape success. Specifically, Doctor Carol S. Dweck outlines what an influential mind houses: fortitude, resilience, and fearlessness. She explains the differences between two very different mind-sets that oppose each other on a spectrum of maturity: fixed and growth.

A fixed mind-set fears failure, believes biology is everything, and thinks hard work is pointless. A growth mind-set loves failure, believes change is always happening, and knows that hard work is essential to find success. I particularly enjoy this read and keep it with me because it not only reminds me that everything will be okay, but it reminds me that for a better future, all I can do is try my best right now and push myself to my limits. Every moment is an opportunity for growth, no matter how it ends up, what it creates for you, or where it takes you emotionally, mentally, or physically (Dweck 2016).

In this way, our lives are neither dictated by our nature nor our nurture but rather by our minds, how we choose to live, and what we choose to do.

Jim Kwik, the founder of KwikLearning.com, a leader in brain performance and accelerated learning for students in over 150 countries, mentioned during *On Purpose* with Jay Shetty that our lives are a summation of all the choices we make until a certain point. He mentions:

"Difficult times can diminish us, distract us, or develop us" (Shetty 2022).

Because of this, our response to adversity genuinely determines our fate. The nature of our minds is critical in deciding what comes next. Limits in life always make us feel safe. Kwik points out that our nervous systems are not set up for this reason; we are afraid to jump because it can be debilitating and harmful and cause a "fight or flight" response. He asserts that life is problematic for two reasons: Either you are leaving your comfort zone or staying stuck in your comfort zone (Shetty 2022).

Kwik outlines a great path to move forward in life that connects well with Dweck's growth mind-set: stretch, stabilize, sacrifice, surrender, and let go. Furthermore, reflection is a powerful tool to overcome limitations, as hindsight can inspire foresight. This specificity in your life to follow a path that connects directly to your heart will allow you to live your truth, ultimately enabling your nature to thrive. In his book, *Limitless: Upgrade Your Brain, Learn Anything Faster, and Unlock Your Exceptional Life* (2020), Kwik describes a triangle connecting three corners: mind-set, motivation, and methods. Mind-set and motivation come together to create inspiration. Mind-set and methods come together to create ideation. Motivation and methods come together to create implementation. Lastly, all three connect to create integration and identity (Shetty 2022).

Ultimately, when diving into these two concepts of nature and nurture, parallel to the concepts of yin and yang, it is necessary to understand that they are, in fact, complementary and work together in your life to formulate who you are. However, the mind is the most critical aspect, epitomized by each circle's middle dots. Our attitude and the way we utilize our mind trumps whatever nature or nurture we have. Instead, it dictates the manifestation of our nature in nurture in the real world by helping us act out our lives effectively or ineffectively.

Chung-liang Al Huang, the founder and president of the Living Tao Foundation and author of *Embrace Tiger, Return to Mountain* (2011), outlines how the practice of tai chi allows one to embrace opposites and embrace our whole lives to arrive at our very center in his 2012 TEDx Talk at Hendrix College. He reaches high up to the sky and says, "You have the spiritual part of you." Then he puts his hand on his heart and says, "Then you have the emotional part of you—human part of you." Then he reaches as low as he can and says, "Then you have the earthly part of you." All three of these parts come together while practicing tai chi, the physical manifestation of the yin-yang symbol. Doing this stretch represents the act of life, pressing on all the essential facets of your existence to create the most whole being you can be (TEDxTalks 2012).

Wholeness comes from intentionality and purposefully expanding in these critically meaningful ways to arrive at a place where your nature and nurture can go together optimally and powerfully, allowing you to step into yourself and be your authentic self fully and deeply.

During his TEDx Talk, Huang draws multiple circles on many white canvases to create many physical, artistic representations for his audience to take in and learn from. Huang never encloses the circles as he draws them with his giant black paintbrush. Instead, he leaves them open and explains that he does this because enclosing a circle creates an unnecessary limit for yourself or your "scope." He likens this open circle to a halo around an angel's head, explaining that when we remain open with our minds, heart, and wholeness, we are indeed "unlimited" in our scope (TEDxTalks 2012).

In Chinese, Huang points out that the "thinking mind" and the "feeling heart" are the same. He explains this connection with a metaphor involving a flower, where everything comes from the center, and nothing is compartmentalized (TEDxTalks 2012).

I think of "nature" and "nurture" in this same way, coming together in a metamorphosis by harnessing a growth mindset and allowing ourselves to be genuinely authentic. Rather than thinking of it in such compartmentalized concepts such as biology and learning, we must come to understand that every moment is a new opportunity to bring ourselves in a brand-new way that is a representation of us as whole, secure, and not dictated by our genes or the way we were brought up into the world.

CHAPTER 11

TV and Cinema

"I'm digging Batman. I'm digging that balance, that duality. He's always on the edge and trying to balance himself within the rules of what's lawful and justice, and being Bruce Wayne and being Batman."
—ZIGGY MARLEY

Media can dictate how we grow up because of what we consume through stories.

While living in Taiwan, I had no TV, radio, or car. This circumstance meant that the sources I relied on to stay updated on American news were my mobile news applications (e.g., ESPN, NewsBreak, and CNN) and YouTube videos. It was refreshing and challenged my mind to find other ways to entertain. Besides the occasional Netflix show, I rarely delved into TV shows or new movies. I read. I ran. And I mainly focused on teaching, writing, and learning. Ironically, while being isolated from it somewhat, I realized that yin yang is omnipresent within the world's entertainment industry.

Nothing in the world seems to illustrate the power of complements better than the entertainment industry—stories, news, and art. Rich, powerful, engaging, honest, and layered stories always seem to feature either an electrifying dynamic of two sides within the main character blending to curate a pained and overzealous figure or two characters bouncing off one another beautifully and harmoniously. In the news, we also see this: two partners coming together powerfully to portray an enticing and attractive dynamism for public consumption. From cinema to our home televisions, many examples illuminate the power and existence of yin, yang, and duality within real-world storytelling.

Probably most famous is Batman and Robin. Born out of a comic book and perfect for the big screen, Batman and Robin represent a superhero combo many others try to emulate endlessly. According to the 2022 article "25 Comic Duos More Dynamic than Batman and Robin," several powerful combinations rival the allure of Batman and Robin (Fugere 2022).

Recently creating much buzz in Hollywood, Deadpool and Cable from their 2016 blockbuster make quite the killer combination with Deadpool's hilariously "fourth-wall-breaking meta-humor" and Cable's muse of a character coming together as a beautiful pair of anti-heroes that polarize audiences (Miller 2016). Even more intriguing to the big screen, some would say, is the combination of Batman and Superman in 2016, a combination featuring super strength and super skills that is unmatched (Snyder 2016). Then there are Cyclops and Marvel Girl, lovers and one of the first members of the X-Men in 2000. Their love has endured the test of time and led to a beautiful baby boy—Cable (Singer 2000).

Then there is Sam and Twitch from *Spawn* (1997), Todd McFarlane's homicide detectives (my favorite type of character), that face monsters together as a very different yet complementary pair. Twitch is small and a great shooter while Sam is massive and straightforward. Their different personalities make them an irresistible team to look at. The list also includes the *Guardians of the Galaxy* saga, starring Chris Pratt and Zoe Saldaña.

Many more comic book and superhero pairs have captivated young comic book fans for decades and have been interesting enough to take up space in big Hollywood budget films. What remains the common denominator in pushing producers and directors over the edge is the dynamism of the two main characters, who represent complementary forces coming together in duality and unity simultaneously (Fugere 2022).

In cinema, couples have become an epic staple in stories we remember forever that have trailblazed a path forward for depicting a relationship with two lovers who balance each other out while ripping our hearts out. According to a 2020 Insider article by Jason Guerrasio titled "The 56 Best On-Screen Couples of All Time, Ranked," the top five couples on screen are from some of my favorite movies: *Casablanca, Titanic, When Harry Met Sally…, Brokeback Mountain,* and *Gone with the Wind.* In *Casablanca* (1943), the powerful characters played by Ingrid Bergman and Humphrey Bogart make it interesting to watch them separately and together. Similarly, Jack and Rose in *Titanic* (1997) have become synonymous with any love story involving opposites. Jack, played by Leonardo DiCaprio, was famously poor and got a free ticket to board the boat. Kate Winslet was wealthy and on the ship with her family and fiancé. The attraction epitomizes the cliché of "opposites attract."

Then, there is Meg Ryan and Billy Crystal in *When Harry Met Sally...* (1989), a beautiful portrait of best friends turning into lovers, causing them to ruin their friendship. *Brokeback Mountain* (2005) is a story of cowboys, played by Jake Gyllenhaal and Heath Ledger, who have a secret love affair, inspiring a string of gay love stories connected to nature in cinema involving two strong male characters who fall in love. Clark Gable and Vivien Leigh play lovers in a toxic affair in *Gone with The Wind* (1939), attached while ruining each other simultaneously (Guerrasio 2020).

The lasting effect of these movies is often inspired by the ripple of the powerful connection between these two characters, displaying a relatable and intense relationship that is hard to forget. The love between these two characters lives at the center of these films as chi lives at the center of us, anchoring and providing stability.

Linn Rivers, a conscious media producer and director based in West Hollywood, discusses yin and yang on screen (in a one-on-one interview with me): "The reality is, though, you cannot have a movie without the yin/yang dynamic. Imagine having two characters on screen who have the same level of strength, the same level of emotional intelligence, and the same level of anger. The movie would never go anywhere as there would never be any resolve. One character would have to drop into the opposite energy in order for anything to come to a conclusion of some sort."

Cinema often mirrors real life, and real life informs the best films because it allows us to relate to and feel deeply connected with characters that experience similar extremes. Rivers continues, "It is beautiful to watch the yin/yang dynamic flip so much in the world of film because that is very true to the way most people live their lives. If they are living in the flow and not trying to overpower every situation, they will find themselves flowing between the spectrum of yin and yang."

One of the greatest stories adapted into shows and movies is Robert Louis Stevenson's *The Strange Case of Dr. Jekyll and Mr. Hyde,* first published in 1886. In my AP literature class in high school, I wrote a creative piece detailing the brutal dismantling Mr. Hyde performed on an older man by bringing him home, killing him, hiding him, and drinking his blood before waking up as an innocent doctor.

Stevenson's book has become one of the most famous stories depicting duality through the lens of dissociative identity disorder, where the victim expresses themselves in two or more uncontrollable personalities. This phenomenon is a severe condition today that has been diagnosed and further illustrated within famous movies on the big screen, such as *Split,* a 2016 thriller featuring a main character with twenty-three distinct personalities. During Stevenson's publication in 1886, DID was not a diagnosed condition, so Stevenson was playing with the idea of a person with an alternate personality, carrying two distinctly different sides within.

There is no evidence that the principle of yin yang inspired Stevenson. Still, his story directly overlaps almost perfectly with light and darkness playing together within us. Doctor Jekyll, a kind-hearted and compassionate doctor, represents yang, active and contributing to society. Mr. Hyde represents darkness, an aggressive monster hidden inside Doctor Jekyll that he has no idea about. The story of these two characters inside of one man as a dualistic dynamic has become a staple in the entertainment industry (Stevenson 2016).

The underlying theme of Stevenson's story is that both a good and bad part exists in all humans. This combination can also be interpreted in many ways—sweet and sour, friendly and aggressive, cautious and impulsive. The difference between the stories' interplay between characters and yin yang is that yin yang is not a combination of productive and destructive but rather a complementary mix that brings out the best in the whole. The disoriented divide of the man who is both characters does not seem to find unity with both. The concept of his two sides thrilled storytellers for years, nonetheless, appearing in several iterative movies using the same title and featuring the same characters. The thrill is that the protagonist and antagonist both live inside the same person. It is confusing, complicated, and always exciting. The franchise is probably one of my favorite representations of dualism inside one person in cinema and television history—all inspired by one book (Stevenson 2016).

Back home in Los Gatos, California, from Los Angeles, I watched a few movies and the morning news with my family while sipping coffee. It was mid-July, and my family and I decided to see *Thor: Love and Thunder* on the big screen. It was intriguing that even the title mirrored two opposing forces: love and thunder. I then discovered *The Man of Tai Chi* (2013), Keanu Reeves's directorial debut. The incredible film featured Mandarin, English, and Hong Kong Cantonese and was released in China before the United States. The fact that Reeves, known for blockbusters such as *The Matrix* and *John Wick*, dedicated a lot of time to a story revolving around tai chi and Asian culture illustrates the yin-yang symbol's relevance to popular culture and perhaps its intrigue. Specifically, the main character's tai chi skills allow him to create a life for himself. The whole story's livelihood and subject matter revolved around the importance and possibility tai chi offers in this Chinese community.

Delving further into meditation and finding balance, *Eat Pray Love* (2010) with Julia Roberts is a home run for illustrating the power of mindfulness. I watched it for the first time while living in Taiwan in the fall of 2022. Based on Elizabeth Gilbert's memoir of the same name, the story follows a woman who rediscovers her self-worth and happiness by traveling to Italy, India, and Bali. In Italy, she feeds her soul through food; in India, she feeds her soul through prayer and silent meditation; and in Bali, she feeds her soul through love.

This movie has come to represent what the power of self-discovery and self-love can do to someone who may feel lost or helpless even in the face of monetary success. Ultimately, Gilbert's connection to prayer and meditation in India is where she achieves a sense of balance and authentic happiness—so much so that she is ready to fall in love again (Murphy 2010).

Perhaps a movie that recently delves into relationship code-pendency more than any other successful movie is *A Star Is Born* (2018), directed by Bradley Cooper. The yin-yang symbol within the relationship between Ally, played by Lady Gaga, and Jackson Maine, played by Bradley Cooper, reaches a crescendo of yang when Ally seems to eclipse Jack's success.

Jack is an old rock artist who struggles with drugs, and Ally helps him recover. Ally, a shy singer, becomes a star with the help of Jack's industry knowledge and advice. Jack is the yang to Ally's yin; the pair is enchanting to watch. However, when Ally begins to outshine Jack and seemingly throws off this balance, the yin-yang homeostasis is also thrown off. Ally no longer needs Jack to be a successful musician, but Jack still needs Ally to stay sober. In the end, this stark imbalance causes Jack to commit suicide (Cooper 2018).

Besides movies, my family and I also watch a lot of morning television, from *Good Morning America* and *Today* to *LIVE with Kelly and Mark*. What we love watching the most is the complementary aspects of the hosts, who each have unique perspectives. For instance, on *Good Morning America,* we love watching Michael Strahan, George Stephanopoulos, and Robin Roberts discuss their opinions from different and diverse perspectives.

On *Today,* my mom loves watching Hoda and Jenna with their glasses of wine, discussing popular culture, their personal lives, and dealing with getting older. We also enjoy watching *LIVE with Kelly and Mark* because their discussions are constantly so enjoyable due to their funny bickering carried along by their humor and differences. Whether it be the female and male dynamic, the old and young dynamic, or the relaxed and hyper dynamic, talk shows are intriguing when there is more than one person involved. Talk shows are always more fascinating when more than one person is involved because the vibration is always collectively raised. Even Jimmy Kimmel has Guillermo, and Jimmy Fallon has Steve Higgins to bicker back and forth with and bounce jokes off of. This balancing is crucial for success, mimicking the Chinese symbol created in BCE.

Lastly, and most importantly, cartoons feature some of the most significant pairs in the history of the entertainment industry, displaying the incredible power of complements to children worldwide. One such pair is SpongeBob and Patrick from one of the greatest animated shows in television history, playing continuously on Nickelodeon since my 2000 birth. The dynamic between the two best friends is contagious and makes you want to laugh every time they hang out.

Similarly, Mickey Mouse and Minnie Mouse are two animated characters from the inception of Disney that have carried an epic tale of friendship in animation. Now, they walk around Disneyland taking pictures with kids from around the world—Mickey representing boys and Minnie representing girls.

Winnie-the-Pooh, the honey-eating bear, has his best friend, Piglet, who he confides in and balances out with his kindness and confidence and Piglet's selflessness and timid nature. Ultimately, the beauty of these animations is the purity of the two characters, who come together beautifully to represent complementary forces perfect for children to enjoy and learn from.

Whether on the big screen or television, the yin-yang symbol is demonstrated deliberately repeatedly in the form of friends, lovers, or working partners. Relationships are paramount to storytelling, and the relationship between two characters captures the beauty of compromise, accommodation, and unity that makes real life worth living.

Several movies and shows depict love and sex. Several people will base their fairy tale love on the romantic comedies and love they like to watch. Unfortunately, this sometimes creates a perfect illusion.

CHAPTER 12

Love Is a Game

———

"Clouds come floating into my life, no longer to carry rain or usher storm, but to add color to my sunset sky."
—RABINDRANATH TAGORE, STRAY BIRDS

I have had many romantic relationships in my life. People close to me know this. I love love. I enjoy experiencing this quality of life, whether it be an emotion, action, or feeling. Any type of love thrills me. Love enables the world to flow and the yin yang within each of us to flow naturally and beautifully. It is beautiful to see the unity within couples who are in love. It is equally intriguing to see the disunity between teams who are not in love.

My first experience with true love was in high school. It was passionate and all-encompassing. Yet it was toxic, emotionally abusive, and hurtful. When the attachment was pure, the relationship flowed naturally. However, the relationship's flow became nonexistent once the love turned into lust, jealousy, and anger. It was challenging for me to continue in such a dizzying imbalance. This type of imbalanced love has occurred frequently in my life. Sometimes, I feel it is a product of true love; other times, I think it may be a product of sin taking over.

Love is blissful, heavenly, interconnected, and full of sorrow, disappointment, and loss at the same time. It is hard to love entirely and even harder to stay committed to someone other than yourself for a long time. Love is full of duality: a side that is happy and giddy and another that can be negative and disastrous. The desire for unity with someone else merges the two. The yang (light) can be found within pure, full-of-heart passion, and the yin (darkness) can be found within hurtful obsessiveness and jealousy.

A relationship can also be full of love or lacking love. I have been on both sides of that coin: constantly thinking about a relationship and letting go of relationships while losing any genuine care for that person. While mutual love is strong with someone else, unity and duality are merged. Unity naturally creates positives and negatives, driven by a strong desire for the other person. True love represents the intermingling of unity and duality, existing without dissension.

In my life, I have had the privilege of experiencing many different types of love. In Addison Aloian's 2022 *Women's Health* article titled "The Eight (Yes, Eight) Types of Love, Explained by Relationship Experts," she outlines the eight types of love that intersect with Greek terms I came to learn while being enamored by psychology in high school: Enduring Love (pragma), Universal Love (agape), Self-Love (philautia), Obsessive Love (mania), Passionate Love (eros), Playful

Love (ludus), Deep Friendship (philia), and Familial Love (storge).

Passionate love is companion-led love, experienced with a true romantic partner. Philia is love between a true friend who is a supporter and a true equal. Playful love is a childish and energetic type of love. This love is a teenage dream type of love and probably my favorite to experience. Universal love is all-encompassing, placing attention and care in everyone's hands no matter who they are or where they come from. Enduring love builds over time with nature, slow and steady. Self-love is personal grace and accountability and is probably the most important in today's hypercritical world. Familial love is a deep blood-related love rooted in being related by blood and having each other's backs. Obsessive love or mania may be the only negative type of love represented by the eight categorical types, as it can drive the obsessor mad (Aloian 2022).

In my lifetime, I would break my love down into four main categories: platonic, romantic, familial, and divine. I like to surround myself with many friends who can teach me about the world through their viewpoints and perspectives. I love soaking up their knowledge and all they have to offer me. I would describe love as "ludus," or fun and childish in all my romantic partnerships. Still, my earlier relationships tended to lean more toward mania on both ends.

Mania is a trait many young relationships tend to have, rooted in lust and obsession versus genuine care, thoughtfulness, and presence. Hopefully, my future relationships will be steeped in "pragma" and fulfilling care for the other person rather than romance or yearning for someone to make me feel better and grant me the attention I want.

Familial love has always been strong in my life, as my family has given me a sturdy base to depend on for unconditional support and validation. I know I can trust my family in any dire situation to be there for me or to calm me down.

Lastly, and probably the most essential aspect of my life, is the divine love in my life, inspired by my Christianity and close relationship with God. God, in my life, plays a significant role, reminding me that I am human and everyone else is also human, and we are all made in the same image and likeness of him. I think my newly formed relationship with him, which continues to develop with each passing day, is crucial because it allows me to keep calm and be brutally honest with myself, my flaws, and where I need to place my attention.

I think the love game comes into play in my life when I try to achieve a balanced time within love:

How much time do I devote to myself versus others?

How much attention given to one person is too much attention?

How can I put God before everyone and please my friends and family?

How can I love myself just as much as everyone else?

Is there a specific time requirement in each department?

Should more time be given to romantic partners or platonic partners?

These are all questions I ask myself when trying to balance the time management of love. It can be very tricky and highly convoluted, blurred by personal desires for one dimension of the love in your life to be louder and fuller than the other dimensions. It is exceptionally critical to give time to yourself to outline the possible positives and negatives of the love you have in your life. Positives can be as simple as happiness and excitement. Negatives may distract you from yourself and your work. Love can be too strong and pull us unfairly from our to-do list as it uncontrollably takes up our subconscious mind. Being self-aware of the yin-yang balance within the love in your life is critical to moving forward with healthy emotional regulation, devoid of love bombing and narcissistic behavior.

It was a windy and cold December morning, the day after I returned from a wildly fun service camp on Lambai Island or Xiaoliuqiu, a coral island in the Taiwan Strait, just south of mainland Taiwan, which included teaching a class as Santa Claus with Ginny McDaniels before a three-hour riotous experience at Oh Ho Bar, sitting next to Robin Hu (soon-to-be Harvard medical student) and a group of bright Fulbrighters from all over the United States on a bunch of cushioned bean bags, discussing the meaning of life drunk. I was still recovering from a weekend including two "Honey Swamp" cocktails or what our Taiwanese waiter insisted we call "Pussy Swamp," encouraged to order from my fellow

Fulbrighters from Oh Ho Bar, From the Sea and Rainbow Sweetheart cocktails from Zoy Thai Thai, a Shoreside cocktail from Shoreside Bar, and a couple of Taiwan Beers from a local BBQ restaurant.

It seemed perfect timing to connect with a spiritual intuitive and Psychic Guide based in Las Vegas named Xyla Divine. I visited a psychic near Rodeo Drive in Beverly Hills and was impressed with the results. Speaking to Xyla, I was excited to get her to take on personal peace of mind and mindfulness in promoting overall wellness within someone's life while also helping her lead a life of spirituality herself.

Love often comes down to a mind-set, perpetuated or hindered by how one takes in their environment. Similar to how stress is very much self-imposed, love can also be determined by the self. You can accept it with open arms or push it away. When discussing the balance between spirituality, balance, and self-love, Xyla discussed forgiveness as being essential. Forgiving yourself and others around you is paramount to continued success and peace in your life. Of course, we need to strive to reach the highest heights we can, but loving and allowing yourself to fall short is also important. Proper balance comes from knowing who you are and accepting it wholeheartedly without a doubt in your mind. When this balance is achieved, loving comes naturally. The importance of fluidly giving and receiving love cannot be understated.

In Clifford Williams' brilliant book *Religion and the Meaning of Life*, he dives into the life-and-death consequences of expressing and accepting love. Specifically, Williams studies suicide and what prevents people from ultimately following through. Williams tackles the four topics that give our lives meaning: achieving goals, creativity, exemplifying virtues and emotions, and love given and received. Of these four topics, Williams wanted to discover what ultimately stopped people from taking their life. In every circumstance, the life-saving factor was love: love given and received (Williams 2020).

Depression and anxiety can cause people to forget about the positive aspects of life. All it takes is a little love to turn that all around. A sense of belonging and understanding that people need and want you is so important. When someone is lost and hopeless, an act of kindness or expression of warmth can be the one factor blocking an unfortunate death. The purpose of mindfulness and self-love is to reach a point where this love is not needed from the outside world but instead bursts within you, giving you life. Find meaning by developing a routine of wellness based on self-love. Because, unfortunately, not everyone can be saved by someone else. We need to find coping strategies ourselves.

It is also interesting to discover that everything has levels and layers—from mindfulness to love. Xyla went on a one-month mindfulness journey, where she took off from work to be silent by herself. This intentional decision allowed her to reprogram her brain and restart how she loved and emitted energy into the world. Xyla defines our emitted energy as frequencies: "We create our reality through our own thoughts, words, feelings, and actions. All these are frequencies. Every frequency has two ends, just like a rope. Whatever you are thinking is a frequency you are emitting loud and clear." This frequency then attracts frequencies just like it.

Furthermore, love is more bound to happen with two frequencies vibrating at similar levels. It is vital to take advantage of this frequency and understand that we have the opportunity to radically change how we deal with the game of love and life by simply changing our mind-set. Life is concise, and so is any "game" in the real world, so the critical piece is to pamper your mind, body, and soul so your spirit is the best it can be during the whole game rather than simply at halftime.

Yin and yang demonstrate the light and darkness in the soul or "chi," which we show the world. Xyla calls this energy "mana" or "a spiritual power, authority or energy within people, places or things," according to the Oxford Dictionary (Oxford Advanced Learner's Dictionary 2015). Xyla explains that "the dark ones" are constantly held inside their ego and show us how not to behave. They are so self-concerned that their love is not genuine or fully present. We agreed that the light, spirit, or true self is far from this ego-driven mania. Xyla explains that different sides of the body are as diverse as different shades: the left is masculine and yang, and the right is feminine and yin. As we swing from each side like a pendulum, it is essential not to go too far right into service for ourselves or too far to the left into service for others. It is hard to connect to our true inner selves if we are on either side, feeding our ego or allowing ourselves to be torn apart. Xyla and I agree that judgment is another form of separation from a genuine love of self and others.

Oxford Learner's Dictionary outlines six definitions of the word "love." Four involve a relationship of some kind, one is a nickname, and one is a score of zero in tennis. The subjects of the four definitions are divided up into "liking and caring," "romantic," "pleasure," and "somebody you like." By the sound of these definitions, most people want to have some form of love, whether it is friendly or more than that. Love makes us smile and makes us happy and gives us a sense of purpose (Oxford Advanced Learner's Dictionary 2015).

To fully step into self-love and acknowledge the intricacies of love, we must be aware of who we are, what we want, and the positives and negatives of the love we have in our lives. Love is not always bright and healthy. Love can be dark and frustrating, leading us down regretful paths of destruction. Find a way to balance the love you give yourself with the love you give others, and life will begin to open up nicely for you in ways you never would have expected. Love is never easy; to fully experience it, one must take a leap of faith to embrace all it can offer. The beauty in taking that leap is witnessing the synergy of unity and duality simultaneously, where two people can align with great intentions, harnessing the masculine and feminine energies within themselves to build each other up.

Even though it may be a game, it is fun to watch and experience when played right. So figure it out and find a balance within yourself to experience love the way it should be.

We are all searching for a complementary pair, and sometimes we need a third-party source to help us get there, such as a therapist, self-help, or even astrology.

CHAPTER 13:

Astrology: Written in the Stars

———

"Millionaires don't need astrologers, but billionaires do."
—JOHN PIERPONT (J.P.) MORGAN

Yin yang is present in astrology study because astrology encompasses opposite yet complementary signs. As people and all organisms contain a balance of yin and yang, specific people are also born under a particular zodiac sign depending on the location and timing of their birth. Furthermore, when coming to Asia, I learned that zodiac signs in Asian culture, represented by animals, are described as either a yin or yang sign.

As previously mentioned, I have a fascination with space. On my ceiling at home, I put glow-in-the-dark stars when I was young. I often thought about parallel universes and daydreamed about what the other me would be doing and thinking in that universe. It lit up my mind. The idea of planets, stars, the sun, and the moon all intrigued me and enabled me to understand that life is so much bigger than just me. It also allowed me to understand that we are all connected and intertwined with the same energy—what I now understand as chi, or the life force energy that flows through us and the world.

Sometimes, what is written in the stars becomes a reality on Earth. I have always been interested in astrology because of the minute details it reveals that often help explain why people are the way they are or why certain people connect easier than others.

Many people disapprove of astrology, believing it is a hoax and made-up baloney. Some of it is overblown. However, it offers revealing layers into our personas, allowing us to truly understand what makes us who we are and why we get along with different people.

Within astrology, we are all given different sun signs, moon signs, and planet placements within the twelve astrological signs (in order from April to March): Aries, Taurus, Gemini, Cancer, Leo, Virgo, Libra, Scorpio, Sagittarius, Capricorn, Aquarius, and Pisces.

According to a 2022 *Today* article by Lisa Stardust, the resident astrologer for *Oprah Magazine* and *Teen Vogue*, people approach life and love differently based on their planetary placements. However, compatibility is based on more than your sun sign because the sun governs the way we shine in the world. At the same time, the moon is connected to our interior landscape, and Venus is related to how we love. Each planet impacts a different aspect of our life (Stardust 2022).

Regarding compatibility, two people usually mesh well when their sun signs are from the same element in the zodiac because they typically have similar values and approaches to life. The earth signs are Taurus, Virgo, and Capricorn. The air signs are Gemini, Libra, and Aquarius. The water signs are Cancer, Scorpio, and Pisces. The fire signs are Aries, Leo, and Sagittarius (Stardust 2022).

An exciting rule also exists called "the sextile rule," which means that signs sixty degrees apart usually form close bonds. For instance, Aries typically get along with Gemini, and Aquarius and Taurus usually get along with Cancer and Pisces (Stardust 2022).

Thinking about yin and yang when thinking about astrology is interesting because it connects to the standard behavior and tempers within each element. Water signs are known to be very emotional and quiet, while earth signs are often very grounded and down to earth. Fire signs are known to be aggressive, passionate, and go-getters. Air signs are known to be very flexible and communicative. Earth and water represent yin because they are connected to the ground, naturally more realistic, and usually easier to decipher. Fire and air represent yang as they are elusive, constantly moving, more upbeat and enthusiastic, and hard to control and predict. Frequently people born within the same element become best friends, but it can sometimes be challenging when both have the same demeanor, as balance within the relationship could be tricky.

For instance, I was born on the first day of the Virgo zodiac sign, also considered the last day of Leo to many, and I have several friends who are fire signs and earth signs. However, sometimes when two people from fire signs are together, both people will want to take the lead and be in charge. This dynamic can, unfortunately, create conflict. Growing up, I would fight a lot with my friends because I am naturally confident in my opinion and what I believe to be true. Sometimes, it is beneficial to have two different temperaments, one from yin and one from yang, so balancing the relationship can work better.

According to a 2022 Well and Good article by Erin Bunch, the zodiac sign is broken down into three parts: polarities (yin/yang), triplicities (fire/earth/air/water), and quadruplicities (cardinal, fixed, and mutable). The positive or yang signs are fire and water, and the negative or yin signs are Earth and air. Astrologer and intuitive healer Rachel Lang describes the intersection and meaning of yin and yang polarity and zodiac signs well:

> "Positive signs tend to focus [energy] outward and be more self-expressive, while negative signs tend to focus their energy inward and be more receptive" (Bunch 2022).

Naturally, yang signs need more attention and action and are usually more outgoing. Yin signs are receptive and take life as it comes, generally planning life rather than acting compulsively. According to Lang, positive signs have an easier time moving from one situation to the next. In contrast, negative signs usually have difficulty letting go (Bunch 2022).

According to the 2022 article by *The Sun*, yin and yang represent the creation of ancient Chinese philosophy, and all Chinese zodiac signs have a yin and yang. The Chinese zodiac has twelve signs named after different animals that correlate with each year rather than monthly. Unlike the four elements used to group American zodiac signs, the Chinese zodiac elements include five: earth, wood, fire, metal, and water. Every sign in the Chinese zodiac has a yin or yang element and one of the five elements attached to it. The yang signs are monkey, tiger, rat, horse, dragon, and dog. The yin signs are rooster, rabbit, pig, snake, ox, and goat. Within this Chinese zodiac chart, compatibility triangles are connected by their polarity. The first triangle is the yang rat, dragon, and monkey. I am a yang dragon because I was born in 2000. The second triangle is yin ox, yin snake, and yin rooster. The third triangle is the yang tiger, horse, and dog. The fourth triangle is the yin rabbit, goat, and pig (Rizzo 2022).

A 2022 article on Lifestyle Asia explains that the study of the five elements in the Chinese zodiac is called Wu Xing, which holds a special place within feng shui and how these elements control and affect our lives. To uncover your element in the Chinese zodiac, you must look at the last digit of your birth year: metal is zero and one, water is two and three, wood is four and five, fire is six and seven, and earth is eight and nine. The metal element represents autumn, rigidity, and strength. The water element represents winter, creativity, and flexibility.

The wood element represents spring, encouragement, and enthusiasm. Fire represents summer, passion, and impulsiveness. Earth symbolizes the yin and yang combination in the transition between seasons, representing dependability and balance (Kulkarni 2022).

While diving deeper into the stars' meaning within our lives is interesting and relevant, it is also important to realize that life has twists and turns and is often unpredictable. As much as having many relationships with both polarities sounds beautiful and balanced, we often must find balance with people from the same polarity because they may relate to us better. Either way, astrology, which has become increasingly popular today, is a fixture in popular culture with horoscopes in all the major newspapers, psychics opening practices around the country, and astrologers sharing their insights through books.

My parents are fire signs. My dad is a Leo, and my mom is an Aries. I think this interesting dynamic in the house helped me push myself to find my sense of fire inside of me—a flame burning with creativity and a need for attention and love. From a young age, I recognized that I loved being surrounded by fire and air signs because those people lit me up and made me feel alive. Like my parents, I only felt at home with people who challenged me and wanted to go on adventures.

According to a 2016 article by Compatibility Zodiac, a combination of a yin zodiac sign and a yang zodiac sign is like butter: The flirting between the two of you makes everyone jealous. Because you are so different in character, you find yourselves easily attracted to and intrigued by one another.

It is a natural connection because it is like a real-life magnet: expressive (yang) and receptive (yin). A friendship between the pair will be inspirational because each will open the other's eyes (Compatibility Zodiac Admin 2016).

In my life, I have realized that most of my friends who have become couples are either both yin zodiac signs or both yang zodiac signs. Intimacy may be better between people centered on the same side of the circle but have differing balances on yin and yang within themselves.

The most coveted animal sign in Asia is the dragon, and being here for some time, I have realized that people take the signs seriously. Many people strive to have children in the year of the dragon because dragon babies are known to be enthusiastic leaders. When I first arrived at school, I remember that one of the first topics we discussed was zodiac animal signs and how this classification melded with our life story and who we were as people.

The dragon defines my life well, as I am usually quick to start an activity on my own and venture down unexpected paths for the sake of growing myself and experiencing more of what life may have to offer. I am usually very result-oriented and positive, so the dragon matches me well.

Astrology is not always 100 percent correct. Still, it provides an outlet to explore identity further and come to terms with what the universe may be telling us. Sometimes, the stars have a plan or message we need to hear.

While walking around Beverly Hills at the beginning of 2021, I encountered a psychic near Rodeo Drive. I was immediately intrigued because I had always wanted a palm reading. She read my palm and said many things—one being that I am always there for others in my life, but people are usually not there for me very often. She also said I do not let people in quickly because I am hard to love due to always wandering and adventuring. She said I love to travel, but I often move too fast. She said I have a big heart and need to guard it because people can take advantage of it. She said something big in my life would happen that weekend, and that weekend I won a car.

It was wild that she said so many in-depth personal details about myself that I knew were true. Still, I never really admitted it aloud or acknowledged it to myself. It is incredible when someone helps you understand specific details about yourself that you would never genuinely otherwise recognize. Sometimes it takes that microscope analysis to come to terms with different qualities about yourself. That is why astrology and palm readings can empower one to understand themselves on a deeper level than wants and dislikes—getting to know the genuine inner you, how you approach the world, what your subconscious may be battling, what makes you relate to others in this world, and what may be coming in your life.

Astrology has always been a source of connection and entertainment to read about weekly. My friends would lend me books about moon signs, my dad reads the horoscope in the newspaper, usually daily and especially on birthdays, and I often read my daily horoscope on Horoscope.com. Because it is part of pop culture, it is enjoyable and often an interesting conversation starter to discuss personalities, preferences, and relationship types based on different zodiac associations within a room.

Yin and yang permeate through the study of astrology—alluding to the energies of signs, especially in Chinese astrology, and explaining why specific signs may make great pairs while others may not.

Addict Restaurant

Hanging with Peter (One of the Best Under 19 Windsurfers in Taiwan and My Student)

Elementary school visit

Ken from Ken's Kitchen

Ken's Kitchen

Las Adelitas in Tainan

*Long Xing (Dragon Star) Restaurant
with PE Teacher*

*One of Many Student Drawings of Their
Teacher*

Milksha with Gabo

Mailing letters underwater

Mizi's House in Xiaoliuqiu

Massage place I visited often

PE Netball

Reading Club

Penghu Houliao Paradise Road

Radio Station next to American Club with

Shirley Lin

Student Fair

Sunla Bistro (enjoyed their cactus punch)

Tommy Nguyen visiting from Vietnam

Swave Bar (with live music)

Teaching about Soccer & The 2022 FIFA World Cup in Qatar

Tide Land cheers with co-teacher Yuwei

Teaching about Bora Bora with Mr. Tsai

Xiying Rainbow Bridge

PART 3:

NAVIGATING THE DUALISTIC WATERS OF THE WORLD

CHAPTER 14

Five Elements, Five Senses

"Magic is really only the utilization of the entire spectrum of the senses."
—MICHAEL SCOTT, THE ALCHEMYST

My favorite sense is taste. Especially in Taiwan, considered the food capital of Asia by some, the taste is extraordinary. Do not get me wrong. I love my sight, smell, touch, and hearing. But taste offers a particular sensory overload, especially when the food is delicious and unique.

Using these five senses in a new country (I had never been to) has increased my gratitude for their functions and ability to help me find peace, purpose, and raw emotion in the world.

Walking down to Beichen Market at six in the morning to enjoy the taste of warm pumpkin noodles entices my soul and makes me happy. It allows me to develop a routine and a sense of balanced stability throughout my day. Seeing locals setting up their tables with fruit, oysters, vegetables, sushi, or raw fish pushes me to be excited for the day ahead. The sweet, tangy smell of the ocean, seafood, and fresh fruit wakes me. The noise of scooters passing by and hungry people picking out what they want for breakfast or the week lightens me up. And the bags in my hand of the food I purchased allow me to feel the weight of something other than myself. The senses on those mornings relax me and ground me in myself, enabling me to smile with feelings of awe, gratitude, and fullness. Sometimes, however, our senses can overwhelm and cause distress. Once we figure out how to best interpret our senses, we can navigate the world more peacefully and happily.

The five senses and five elements help to navigate the duality of the world because they help us make sense of finding balance within ourselves as we relate to the universe. The five senses enable us to connect to the world through our ability to consume the world through sight, hearing, vision, touch, and taste. The five elements help us understand the world through specificity in clear, definitive classifications: fire, water, earth, metal, and wood. Through these five senses and elements, we can connect the parts of ourselves with the details of the world, literally and figuratively.

In his 2019 video titled "5 Tips to Naturally Cleanse Your Body at Home," Sadhguru discusses the five elements and their essential roles in purification. Every element (earth, water, air, fire, and space) is critical in our lives to flourish and balance ourselves to the best of our ability. I believe it takes addressing and living through all five of our human senses to fully take in the human experience for what it is and correctly cleanse our entire body. Incredibly, Sadhguru explains that 72 percent of our bodies are water, 12 percent is earth, 6 percent is air, 4 percent is fire, and the rest is Akash or "space" (Sadhguru 2019).

To fully embrace this beautiful and magnetic wholeness within and outside us, we must deliberately choose to acknowledge and respect the existence of all of these elements within and around us. Interestingly, we serve as a mirror for the planet, consisting of the same elements, essentially the same stardust—connected and fluid like "qi" or the life force in Daoism, Asian culture, and specifically yin yang ideology.

According to studies by Heisook Kim from Ewha Womans University in Korea, until around the fourth century BC, yin and yang denoted "shade" and "sunshine." In many Eastern cultures, the study of yin and yang and the five phases was dominant until recently.

Understanding the fluidity of yin and yang and the five senses allows one to truly respect the connection between the two forces and the five phases: wood, fire, soil, metal, and water (Kim 2000).

Because yin and yang represent a continuous cycle between masculine and feminine complementary forces, it makes sense why the symbol has come to explain many different processes within the world. Kim specifically looks at phases that mirror the five phases of wood, fire, soil, metal, and water. The domains with these five phases include many relevant and interesting concepts within our world, such as direction, season, viscera, sense organ, color, time, feeling, taste, voice, number, creature, and chi (Kim 2000).

This harmonious world of phases represents the epitome of balance, beauty, and complementary inter-workings. It differs from a world of pure causality, where reactions create actions, and much is uncontrolled. Heisook explains:

"Harmony and order come about in the former as assimilated things grouped together in one of the fives move in ever-lasting cyclic order, whereas in the latter they lie in lawfulness where similar cases are subsumed under a general law" (Kim 2000).

Either way, groupings within different domains of life exist, sometimes acting singularly and sometimes happening haphazardly together but always performing toward a sense of unity between all phases (Kim 2000).

The forces of Yin and Yang help the five phases take continuous action and relate to one another better, like glue or gas. Glue because they help fasten the stages together, and gas because they enable movement from one stage to the next. These two forces are actors in the changing of the phases. For example, yang helps jumpstart spring (the wood phase) and the heat of summer (the fire phase). At the same time, yin accompanies the fall harvest (the metal phase) and the hibernation of winter (the water phase). Perhaps, the soil phase represents the synergy between yin and yang and the grounding of all these seasons in the midst of transforming into one another. Kim denotes soil as late summer—the seamless transition between summer and autumn, the beaming sun and the falling leaves, and yang and yin (Kim 2000).

As I transition between the seasons within the years of my life, this sense of transition naturally happens as I move from one stage to the next. Usually, in winter, I am more stagnant and can relax more. Enjoying the winter season in Penghu, it has been easier for me to slow down, reflect, and take some time to enjoy my solitude. During the summer months, I am usually on the go—hiking, biking, tanning, swimming, and going out every night. The heat naturally makes me more active and excited. I can see why yin correlates to winter and fall and yang correlates to spring and summer. Similar to the rising and falling temperatures, people's motivation usually increases in the spring and summer, the start and middle of the year, and decreases in the winter, the end of the year, to celebrate holidays such as Thanksgiving, Hanukkah, and Christmas with family and friends, reflecting on the year and celebrating. My winter hibernating and personal reflection allow me to prepare and understand precisely what I want to do moving forward the following year. Each new year symbolizes turning a page in my life, shedding the past year, and moving forward with new energy and newfound security from the restful holiday season.

Sadhguru explains that water must be cherished because it takes up seventy-two percent of our body and possesses incredible memory. We should always keep a water vessel next to our beds overnight because it will wake us fresh, cleansed of all the memories of where it may have been the day before. Time is vital to allow the water to prepare for you (Sadhguru 2019).

The Earth denotes eating food. Every aspect of eating is vital—where the food comes from, how you approach it, and how you consume it. This intentionality means cherishing our ability to taste. According to the Isha Foundation's 2021 article, "The Importance of the Element of Earth," earth is the foundation of our physicality and all other elements. Whereas you can transform other elements, earth is stationary and represents who we are and where we have come from. After all, we all come from the planet:

> "We are born of the earth. Our biological mother is only a representative who is also born of the same earth. The real mother is the soil that we carry as our bodies" (Sadhguru 2021).

When we think of our essence as soil, we inch closer to appreciating life's simple aspects by understanding that all our cores are similar. When we recognize our similarities and origins, we can maintain a sense of grounding that allows us to connect to our identity while enhancing our mental state and how we enjoy life. The Isha Foundation explains, "Whenever you eat food, you swallow a part of the earth. Essentially, we take in a part of the planet to sustain the body" (Sadhguru 2021).

However, according to a 2020 *Time* article by Alana Semuels, the UN's report created by more than one hundred experts "warned that exploitation of land and water is already putting pressure on humanity's ability to feed itself." Due to high temperatures and excessive flooding, billions of dollars are invested in companies creating meat and dairy products from plants or cells. Vertical farms are also prevalent now too to maximize plant growth. The more we eat plants, the better our ever-growing population will survive. Eating plants connects us more profoundly with the Earth element and reduces the carbon dioxide emissions from eating meat. Recreating food with plants enables us to do more with less while connecting with Earth in a new way—utilizing soil in skyscrapers and allowing trees to occupy precious land. Plant-based eating may enable us to balance caring for the Earth, our bodies, and climate change, establishing an essential balance needed to navigate the world (Semuels 2020).

Out of that, 6 percent of our bodies are made from air. Less than one percent is the air that we breathe because the air is within our cells. Our muscles and our heart need air and oxygen to function. Air is consistently affected by sounds, intentions, and emotions, so the public easily sways it. As living human beings, we must learn to harness the positive air correctly and not be lost in toxic air that could be tainted with sinful activities. This discrepancy is why nature is so important to explore. The open environment delivers fresh air to nourish our body and mind through our sense of smell. Feeling the cold air move through my nose on a hike is beautiful and like nothing else in the world (Sadhguru 2019).

Sunlight is the purest form of energy we can soak up. The beauty is that no one can tarnish sunlight like air as it comes directly from the sun in space. When we truly value our sense of feeling, we can enjoy the Vitamin D in the world for all it is and offers us (Sadhguru 2019).

Lastly, and most importantly, Sadhguru exclaims to take care of the fire within us and our inner spirit. This care means understanding where our fire burns from—jealousy, envy, greed, hatred, resentment, anger, love, compassion, etcetera (Sadhguru 2019).

Finding yin and yang is centered on intentionally experiencing all of your senses for all they offer. To make this cherishing easier, we can focus on all five elements around us, prioritizing the worth of each one. Take life in for all it offers your five senses; happiness will be almost impossible to escape. When fire is channeled for the right reasons, balance will feel effortless as your spirit will guide your actions from a place of love and appreciation for all God has blessed you with.

Heisook's connection of the elements to the planet's seasons in her work illuminates the idea that our wholesomeness mirrors the wholesomeness of the planet. As we possess all five elements and experience all five senses within ourselves, the planet possesses all five elements and experiences four seasons that each represent an element. The connective tissue these elements represent manifests beautifully within our lives as human beings and within the greater scheme of earth. Fully embracing these elements and our senses enables us to fully experience what the yin-yang symbol represents:

healthy counterparts, essential phases, the critical duality of rest and action, speed and slow, and heat and cold.

According to a brilliant 2022 MindOwl article, we can use all five senses—sound, smell, taste, touch, and sight—to ground ourselves and become more mindful. An activity specifically spotlighted within the article for this universal grounding is the "5-4-3-2-1 grounding exercise." This exercise is quite simple: find a quiet place to be alone, sit up straight, put your hands on your thighs, and take a few breaths before committing one minute to experience each of your senses fully in the silence of your area (Bastos 2022).

Each exercise focused on each sense should take exactly one minute, entirely devoted to enjoying that specific sensory experience without any judgment getting in the way of perceiving what that sense offers you. Toward the end of each minute, you should be able to recognize more of what that sense provides. For example, when listening to your surroundings as you get closer to a full minute, you will likely be able to decipher more of the sounds around you: the clinking of glasses, the closing of doors, the soft music in the background, and all the small conversations happening.

While doing this, it is crucial to realize all the small things that fill up your day and the details in your surroundings that make your senses the way they are. For instance, while smelling, try to decipher the scent of your cologne, your shampoo, the food in the area, the smell of the clean-cut grass, and any other odors that may be around. While looking around, notice colors, shapes, textures, and sizes to ground you in your environment. The trick is to spend only a little time on one scent or sight and move through them smoothly and effectively (Bastos 2022).

Mindfulness and happiness are never too far away when we can find immense gratitude within the specific senses in our everyday lives. This pledge to take in our surroundings with grace and appreciation pushes us past life on a slow back burner and closer to a life lit up by passion and curiosity to fully discover what is in front of us.

When we can fully grasp the human senses defined by humanity, we can unlock what may be beyond these senses—transcending humankind to enter a realm of existence that is divine, hyperaware, and fully formed in mindfulness, adaptability, and love. Deepak Chopra examined along with Menas C. Kafatos, PhD, and Subhash Kak, PhD, in a 2014 article that actual reality pushes beyond any form of humanistic sensing capabilities: "Reality transcends any model we can possibly make of it."

Perhaps he means that true mindfulness transcends how the senses can even make us feel by pushing our past thoughts, emotions, and desires further to a fundamental truth that connects all living beings magically: heart, movement, and pure happiness. Chopra may be referencing what Michael Scott (2019) acknowledges: The senses are mere gateways to the soul, acting as a mechanism to try to understand ourselves rather than fully understanding our reality, which is forever incomprehensible (Chopra et al. 2014).

James Cameron, film director of *Titanic* and *Avatar*, explains his thoughts about creativity and imagination:

"It's about human imagination and curiosity. What's out there? What's in the great beyond? What exists at levels we can't see with our five senses?" (Industrial Scripts 2016).

In storytelling, we can truly revel in the ability of fictionalized tales to empower the possibility of what could be in the real world. I suppose dreaming is where manifestation is created— speaking what you desire into existence. Life is most often what you make of it, created by how you evaluate and perceive your senses and how you carry yourself in your environment.

On Christmas in Taiwan, I sit at Donutes Cafe in Downtown Magong City, Taiwan, reading the New Testament and *Atlas of the Heart* by Brené Brown. I enjoyed a delicious coffee smoothie after making some peanut butter and banana French toast this morning. As I take in my surroundings this Christmas, I understand how blessed I am to be alive and to have the opportunity to grow and nourish my body. I look around and see the many Penghu locals grabbing their holiday coffee, smell baked goods on the shelves, and hear Taiwanese music lightly in the background. In contrast, many families and friends speak in Mandarin to one another. I am content. I am fulfilled. I am so delighted because I have realized that I am alive and can take in everything around me and accept my reality, which can be so much more than what it is based on how I receive it and take advantage of it.

5 Elements, 5 Senses, 1 Life, 1 You. You decide how you want to live.

CHAPTER 15

The Profound Key: Mindfulness

"Breathing in, I calm body and mind. Breathing out, I smile. Dwelling in the present moment I know this is the only moment."
—THICH NHAT HANH, *BEING PEACE*

In the spring of 2021, I was boarding a plane at LAX to fly to Puerto Vallarta in the middle of April during my spring break. I was sitting on the plane, ready to enjoy a beautiful and peaceful flight to a new country. A woman sitting next to me tapped my shoulder.

She asked me, "Are you religious?"

I answered, "Yes. I am a Christian."

She exclaimed, "God has told me something about you. He says you are a healer. I was praying to him, and he told me about you." She gave me a piece of paper with writing on it. I looked down at it. It read:

"You are a natural healer. God will reward your power and dedication to him. Lean into God and the Holy Spirit and stop worrying."

I nearly teared up and wondered how she could tell I was religious. She looked me in the eyes and just smiled. That moment has always stuck with me as an example of the Holy Spirit speaking through people naturally. Throughout the rest of 2021, my relationship with God and meditation strengthened, and so did my ability to positively impact others.

I realized this when Congress rewarded me with a Fulbright scholarship before my 2022 graduation from the University of Southern California. It was a brilliant cherry on top of three years at USC that were challenging, high-spirited, and enchanting. After a fast and delirious summer in California, I flew to Taipei, Taiwan, at the beginning of August 2022 to begin my teaching journey in the first country I have ever visited where Mandarin is the most common language. I then flew to the Penghu islands and settled into an apartment in the capital city, Magong, directly next to the local fresh food market, Beichen Market. It quickly became my cozy home.

Fast forward through many 7-Eleven visits, many ramen meals, and a lot of walking and biking, I obtained a scooter license, a Taiwan bank account, an alien resident certificate, national health insurance, and learned about a year's worth of Chinese culture in what felt like a year but was only three months. On Thursday, October 27, it was midnight. For me, midnight has become my afternoon. Time is no longer a concept in my life as I age. I was putting away my laundry in my brown dresser inside my Taiwanese bedroom, overlooking the busy Beichen market in Magong City, Penghu County. I set up an interview with David Vago, a brilliant former TEDx Speaker who has trailblazed a path in contemplative science. Vago recently returned from an excursion with the Dalai Lama and naturally had a lot on his mind.

What inspired Vago is simple curiosity and a specific intention—trying to make sense of bringing together Buddhist epistemology and the Western mind-brain. As a Christian, the Holy Bible is often used as a connection to the divine through understanding the life of God's son and gaining a greater connection to the Holy Spirit. When speaking to Vago, he expressed how there are often moments of deep meditation in these spiritual books. He said people often lose sight of the true meaning of meditation. It is not a forced activity of attempting to escape oneself. It is a potent activity that allows one to focus on one's mental habits and connect with the nature of the mind.

As Vago and I chatted, we acknowledged the cursed and blessed dichotomy of planet Earth. As a mathematician, studying a system within its own system is impossible. As earthlings, we are both "blessed and plagued with thought." We can think about life's many complexities. Still, we also tend to overthink to the point of inaction or unhealthy judgment of ourselves and others.

When speaking of his work with the fourteenth Dalai Lama, who resides in India, Vago reminded me that Aristotle and other philosophers encourage connecting with the nature of your mind, acknowledging that self-reflection is a fundamental aspect of being human. Vago has a beautiful way of putting meditation:

"Self-regulation of attention with the purpose of gaining insight into the nature of mind or connection with the divine."

Vago identifies as Jewish through familial heritage, and we discussed the intricacies of meditation within each religious practice as well as how it has a place within any spiritual or wisdom tradition. Vago's father was in the Holocaust, which helped Vago develop a strong sense of cognitive empathy. Vago seems to be solid and aware that religion is powerful, appreciating the heritage he has while also expressing himself in his very own way spiritually. Vago practices Pantheism, believing in something bigger than oneself but not necessarily a supernatural God.

A week before we talked, Vago was with the Dalai Lama. Incredibly, the Dalai Lama is gearing up for death. With all his time spent with the spiritual being, Vago says the Dalai Lama recycles a very similar message of importance in life:

"We have to abide by human connection by respecting our differences and highlighting the fact that we are the same."

As a scientist, Vago naturally gravitated toward Buddhism because it acts as less of a dogma and more of a way of life: spirit, soul, or nonself and giving back to humanity. The Dalai Lama is now eighty-seven years old and discussing his death. Naturally, the Dalai Lama says a luminous light surrounds him as the convergence of life and death come together, and he gets ready for reincarnation into his next life. I am happy to join Vago in occupying his space and spreading his message of healing through the mind.

We all carry baggage and deal with mental blocks. I listened to a TCOC (Taiwan Church of Christ) session on Sunday during the weekly 11 a.m. to 12 p.m. window. During the sermon, I heard, "When we think about salvage that God has given us, we can see that the present is so short, but the long future will save us forever." Vago points out that our lives are made up of moments that make up who we are.

Each moment can be defined by short three-hundred- to five-hundred-millisecond moments. These moments and the moments our ancestors have experienced come together to make up who we are. We are all different because of this and our genes. However, we can agree that sleep, faith, and mental strength are crucial for life's success and happiness. Interestingly, the Dalai Lama sometimes calls himself a "Good Christian" as the New Testament's central message is to "love thyself as you love thy neighbor" and clearly distinguish oneself from others.

Doctor Vago and I closed our intriguing discussion with a conversation on balance—between work life, societal norms, spiritual beliefs, and life's many stresses. Vago and I agree that there is no reason to have anxiety when viewing life's moments as opportunities for life. Vago brought up the Buddhist concept of "Poli." Poli translates to "equanimity" or staying neutral in all aspects of life—ups and downs. This concept calls for detachment and remaining calm during stress, war, or extreme pleasure. Vago says that he and Harvard professors measure equanimity by the recovery time someone requires when returning to baseline after an intense emotion. People with high emotional skills have high indicators of equanimity.

Life is full of noise. Intense, hateful noise. Beautiful, pleasurable noise. Noise is primarily a source of distraction. Boundaries are necessary. Personal time is essential. Protection of the heart is paramount. Mindfulness is the profound key to self-love and decisive, authentic action.

I spoke with Doctor William Danaher, who received his PhD in Religious Ethics from Yale University before teaching theology at the University of the South, The General Theological Seminary, and served as Dean and Huron-Lawson Chair of Moral and Pastoral Theology at Huron University College in London, Ontario. He now serves as a rector and priest at Christ Church Cranbrook.

When I asked Danaher to tell me about the power of mindfulness in the simplest of terms, he coolly asserted, "Mindfulness is a practice of becoming present to yourself as a way to cope with different challenges—such as stress, anxiety, and depression—that are part of the fabric of everyday life."

Presence is key. In a religious context, we can be present to God when we are present to ourselves. This presence is a form of self-love, enabling us to see ourselves as God sees us. But presence takes work. It takes attention and energy.

Mindfulness takes authentic intention. John Kabat-Zinn, Professor of Medicine Emeritus at the University Massachusetts Medical School, gave a beautiful speech on April 7, 2011, at The Tucker Foundation and Dartmouth Hitchcock Medical Center at Dartmouth College. His impactful, nearly two-hour lecture was titled "The Healing Power of Mindfulness."

One of the standout lessons of Kabat-Zinn's talk was that people live life often mindlessly, without a sense of direction or purpose. This aimless existence takes us away from so many moments we fail to consume. Kabat-Zinn acknowledges that a lot of people are stuck in the past:

"Our mind is up to memory and things that are already over. Another preoccupation of the mind is on the future" (Kabat-Zinn 2011).

Many people's thoughts about the future are not positive, either. This downward spiral of thinking and mind wandering leads to regret and worry. The fact is, most of the things we worry about as a society never actually happen. Mark Twain captures this expertly in his famous sentiment:

"There has been a huge amount of tragedy in my life, and some of it has actually happened" (Kabat-Zinn 2011).

The funny concept of Earth is that pressure is part of the human condition. It will never be absent in a human being's short life. This unfortunate or fortunate happening (depending on how you view it) means we must remain present no matter how things unfold. After all, if we desire a better future, the only cause for that is the present moment we are living in. The past cannot be altered, and the future is the present moment, second by second, in front of us to take advantage of. Kabat-Zinn exclaims that each moment is a new opportunity to be someone new. He deems it "the art of living our lives as if they really mattered" (Kabat-Zinn 2011).

According to Kabat-Zinn, when we recognize that we can control what is around us and directly change our lives for ourselves, there is a cosmic shift in our perspective and awareness of the world we occupy. Many people repeat the phrase: "Just be." This phrase precisely means that we are defined by who we are, our characteristics and the people we impact, rather than what we constantly do, our achievements or our job. Again, success means surrendering to life's circumstances, or the process, while entrusting yourself and your skills. Kabat-Zinn recognizes this paradox as he speaks about working with Olympic athletes:

> "You cannot improve performance by trying to improve performance" (Kabat-Zinn 2011).

This idea undoubtedly returns to balance. To ultimately be yourself or any character, you must embrace your opposites, imperfection, and ultimately your fate without force. This concept reminds me of acting. When developing a persona, pulling from opposites is completely necessary as it allows one to create a well-rounded human being that people will want to understand and come to know. When delving into a role, an actor usually asks the question: What is the emotional journey of this character, and what is my why (motive)?

When speaking to Director Gil Junger in the summer of 2022 in Los Angeles (director of *10 Things I Hate About You*), he confirmed my belief that the best actors do not read around their lines for direction. Instead, they make the character authentic to who they are—not forced. Not robotic. Just natural. Similarly, when chatting with actor Kevin Scott Allen, he often discussed that thinking gets us caught up in our heads too much, distracting us from marrying the material with who we are.

I like to think of my life as a big, beautiful picture. I can paint it how I want, and in any way I want. To live through myself, I must define my stakes in life and all situations, which means

I must express myself freely and openly while defining all my intentions calmly—whether in my head or aloud.

As Kabat-Zinn puts it, "Nothing happens next, this is it" (2011). True beauty is appreciated in all five of your senses for what they offer you: sight, smell, hearing, taste, and touch. Live a life that enjoys these senses deliberately and thoroughly. Frequently, people admit their terror of death, but what if this is being scared of yourself and your purpose? Awareness and meta-awareness are the steps to learning and healing the process of growing up as a human being. Recognize your beauty and come to your senses. Allow yourself to physically, metaphorically, and figuratively come to life.

Appreciate the stillness. Appreciate the excellent day and moment you are in as you read this word. This moment will become *part* of "the good old days" and history forever.

CHAPTER 16

Ignite the Love: The Power of Self-Love to Love Others

"If you want peace, you don't talk to your friends. You talk to your enemies."
—DESMOND TUTU

Calmness. A tree with roots. An endless grass field to play on. I see the soccer field as I sit at my desk at Peng Nan Junior High School, preparing to meet with the principal, my LET (Local English Teacher), and two other teachers. We meet every Monday to review my morning international education class and discuss the week ahead for each class: seventh-grade English, eighth-grade English, ninth-grade English, physical education, international education, and reading club. The meeting is usually short and sweet, discussing successes and specific moments where we can all improve to ensure the learning environment and teaching are always at the highest level possible.

I usually catch up on the morning news through YouTube and update myself on current events. Today, it is all about Elon Musk buying Twitter: capitalism bleeding into our social media. It is also Halloween today, and I am dressed as coffee—a medium roast with half and half and a dollop of whipped cream. I then listen to podcasts to balance my morning and ease me into the day. *On Purpose* with Jay Shetty has been a constant source of wisdom to stay grounded and hear about people's stories of resilience and perseverance. I believe there is enormous power in finding self-love through understanding how others have seen it and how to find a place of true healing.

In an *On Purpose* with Jay Shetty podcast interview on December 21, 2020, musical artist, Jhené Aiko, discusses the power of contemplation and observation. These two activities are powerful in uncovering your true inner self. Aiko, a remarkably down-to-earth individual, talks about her fascination with life and death and how grieving her brother's death and experiencing her daughter's birth were soul-searching and spiritual (Shetty 2020).

Meditation in Aiko's life has allowed her to write simple and poetic writing. Meditation enables her to feel spiritually, mentally, and physically better. She practices the "Red Light Meditation," taught by Vietnamese monk Thich Nhat Hanh (Shetty 2020), widely considered to be "The Father of Mindfulness," according to his foundation's website (Thich Nhat Hanh Foundation 2023).

This meditative practice encourages taking a breath at each red light while driving. Aiko channels this calming energy into her beautiful music. At a spiritual store, she found sound bowls and used them in her most recent Grammy-nominated album, *Chilombo*. Like my purpose, Aiko has realized that her life's purpose is to heal others and help them deal with their lives. She wants to create music to encourage intention and recovery to resonate within your body and spirit to center and ground yourself.

Life becomes so rich when one finds meaning in the people and places around them. When life is this rich, being in touch with your inner voice is much easier, allowing one to be at peace, surrender, and truly let go. When you permit yourself to move freely, you liberate yourself from constraints and opinions. Loving and appreciating the Earth's beauty allows you to love your beauty and express it in your unique way. There is power, knowing there is no right or wrong. The status quo is meant to be broken, so do not feel compelled to limit yourself (Shetty 2020).

Dinesh Chandra, cofounder of The Global Integrative Wellness Network and successful worldwide transformational coach, has worked with many of the world's top companies in fifteen different countries and co-edited a book entitled *What is True Wealth & How Do We Create It* after meeting with His Holiness the fourteenth Dalai Lama.

When I asked him what self-love means, he replied, "Self-love means unity consciousness where self includes all." Unity consciousness is a beautiful expression that captures the essence of the power of self-love in helping to love others.

When one can let go and be a present witness, spirituality represents pure love that is always balanced and unshakable next to any earthly material.

Self-reflection and returning to your roots are essential to thriving in the world. Restoration, reflection, and connection with the center of who you are allow you to gauge your purpose and whom you want to become.

FINDING THE DEEPEST LOVE FOR YOURSELF IS TO HEAL OTHERS
World-renowned holistic health practitioner Linn Rivers and I discussed the relationship between spirituality, balance, and self-love. We both agree that they are completely intertwined and cannot be separated. Rivers states, "You cannot fully immerse yourself in anything outside of yourself until you truly find the deepest love for yourself. I think so many people are afraid of being alone because they have not found that relationship with self."

I agree wholeheartedly with Rivers because managing themselves and other relationships takes a fully formed, self-accepting, and truly healed person. When the relationship with yourself is found, all other connections are a beautiful bonus.

Rivers continues: "You may find yourself through spirituality, but you also find a deeper sense of spirituality through finding yourself. They go hand in hand. Once you find that, the balance automatically comes into play. You make yourself a priority."

My journey with self-love has been a windy and challenging road. I grew up in Los Gatos, in the same home my whole life, next to the Santa Cruz mountains. Life was a constant adventure for me. I played five sports growing up: basketball, baseball, football, soccer, volleyball, and more, on top of that, recreationally. I attended public elementary and middle school before attending a private Catholic high school. As a child, I was a perfectionist. In everything I did, I wanted it to be perfect—from my writing to my teaching to my performances on the sports field or in the classroom. Naturally, I developed stressful anxiety in everything I did because I always felt nothing would be good enough. Once I finally reached high school and was introduced to religion, I began to see the power of prayer, solitude, and rest. However, I maintained unmatched energy and enthusiastically went after different opportunities restlessly. This ambition never faded when I attended the University of Southern California. I double minored while majoring in business.

When I decided to get rebaptized in Santa Monica and take control of my relationship with God, I realized my whole life I had been overflowing my table with too many things to overcompensate with my insecurity of not doing enough. I realized I would be the same person no matter how much I commit. My life became rich because everything I did started to have much more depth and intention behind it. I felt at peace and no longer needed to extend myself to places. Instead, I just lived.

This transition allowed me to create time for self-care, which looked like massages, baths, watching movies, and reading. Once I realized that life is too short to care about the details and overthink about being the best at everything, I could enjoy every moment and take in my surroundings as I never did before. Have fun and enjoy. Life is too short to stress out over. Everything works out in the end.

When opening up entrepreneurship books like *What I Wish I Knew When I Was 20: A Crash Course on Making Your Place in The World* (2019) by Tina Seelig, I realized that every moment is a rich opportunity in your life. Every person and every physical piece within your life can be altered or thought of differently. Because of this, the past does not matter. The present is where the magic happens. Mindfulness allows us to extract everything we want out of this exact present moment. Be here. Now. There is no better place to be.

IS SELF-WORTH SELFISH?

When presence is engaged at the highest level possible, your ability to be yourself and fully open up and love others is achieved. This dichotomy or paradox is relatively simple yet often inappropriately used in the real world. People either view taking time for themselves as selfish or unnecessary. Instead, it is neither. It is necessary and paramount for high performance by allowing you time to reflect and take care of yourself—two activities needed to maintain wellness.

It pays well to be selfish to be selfless. According to Adia Gooden's 2018 TEDx Talk at DePaul University, the leading cause of sickness and disability is depression. And depression is caused by low self-worth, which is caused by a lack of self-care. In other words, a feeling of despair and unworthiness is often due to relying on external factors for validation rather than finding inner peace. Sometimes, we shouldn't assume it is our fault since the world forces us out of the necessary mind-set toward happiness. This dramatic force may be due to materialistic and capitalistic advertisements, emphasizing that a grade point average equates to your intelligence and the treacherous social media comparison storm. Gooden explains the need for unconditional self-worth:

> "It is time for us to base our worth on the fact that we are human to cultivate a worth that persists even when life does not go as we hoped" (Gooden 2018).

Humans must understand that our self-worth is never at stake because we are alive. There is no fight to be had, but rather a peaceful existence of living your truth and being yourself.

I have struggled with perfectionism and not feeling worthy for much of my life. This undying need to be perfect often paralyzed me and left me questioning my judgment due to past mistakes or beating myself up for not living up to my unfair expectations of myself. Over the years, as I have gleaned ten steps to follow to reach an empowering point of unconditional self-love from the Bible, my higher education, my life's winding journey, and many mentors, both religious and nonreligious. Each step starts with an "F" to symbolize "Faith in the Future."

1. Find excitement in your purpose.

2. Forgive those around you and yourself.
3. Feel all your emotions and accept them for what they are.
4. Follow your heart and do not overthink it.
5. Face your hiccups head-on and learn from them.
6. Feed and nurture the love that exists around you.
7. Form intimate bonds with the people who lift you and are essential to you.
8. Fulfill your promises or plans.
9. Free yourself from any expectations or assumptions.
10. Fear nothing but God.

Many of these steps are interrelated, which is on purpose because they are all intertwined in one way or another through liberating oneself from a box or standard to live naturally. Like many concepts in life, achieving all ten is easier said than done. However, starting with anyone is a fulfilling beginning to a life filled with self-love.

Of course, becoming healthy starts with yourself and no one else. This selfishness to fix your attitude, outlook, and fundamental worldview allows you to perform at a higher level and be there for those around you. Suppose you can be there for yourself when you experience emotional pain and trauma. In that case, you can be there for others sharing that same pain. Love unconditionally by radically accepting who you are and what you offer. Live from within.

Lisa Barnett, international bestselling author and founder of Akashic Knowing School, told me: "Self-love is essential in our well-being as humans. Everyone needs time, space, physical care and self-love to live our soul's purpose."

I hugely agree. To embrace personhood, we must embrace our true selves and love deeply.

She continued, "I think you can't truly be spiritual without balance and self-love." Spirituality breeds acknowledging humanity and embracing the yin-yang symbol's iconography of symmetry, interconnectedness, and wholeness—qualities grounded in sincere love.

I was acclimating to my life in Magong City, Penghu County, when I received news that Michelle Obama would be releasing another book on November 15, 2022 as a follow-up to her book, *Becoming*, which I ordered my mom for Christmas back in 2018. Flash forward to the holiday season in 2020, and I was watching Oprah's 2020 Vision Tour Visionaries, a vision tour for wellness. I watched Michelle Obama speak about a familiar insecurity at the root of a lack of self-love and insecurity: "Am I enough?" (WeightWatchers 2020).

What all of the Visionaries on tour—Obama, Jennifer Lopez, Amy Schumer, Tina Fey, Kate Hudson, Gayle King, Tracee Ellis Ross, Lady Gaga, and Dwayne Johnson—had in common was the ability to accept themselves, be brave, and live authentically from within. A radical discovery in several of their lives was the fact that their life was their own. That simple switch lit a fire in them. Outside noise is nonsense, distracting you from developing your happiness. Start with kindness to yourself and others (WeightWatchers 2020).

Karma is a genuine beast in the world. If you release positivity into the world, more than likely, positivity will come back to you. After releasing my first book during the same month I graduated in 2022, I never thought I would have the impact I had in the entertainment industry. Because of my genuine interest and love for restaurants, I spent time, energy, and brain power writing a book from my heart. My words have inspired many artists after me to write their own book. Ultimately, when you put your love and genuine hard work on display for others to witness and see, people will respond to your work.

The lesson: Follow your heart. More importantly: Nourish your heart's desire, and that nourishment may be recognizable by the world. If not, it will allow you to inspire others to participate in their nourishment. That precious nourishment is all we need and desire to feel fulfilled. Utilize your time wisely and do not waste alone time as a clock does not have empathy, but you do.

CHAPTER 17

Stress Is Self-Imposed. Stop Worrying.

——

"Vulnerability is our capacity to be wounded."
—DOCTOR GABOR MATÉ

Through discussions, Taiwanese temple visits, and sit-downs with Fulbright officials, one common denominator trumps any other card: One must be vulnerable to grow.

I flew to Taiwan abruptly, returning to the San Francisco Bay Area (my hometown) just moments before boarding at the San Francisco Airport. I came from a film project in Los Angeles before packing quickly and saying goodbye to old friends and my family. I landed in Taipei, an extreme beginner at Mandarin, learning day by day how to navigate a new country with no immediate friends next to me. I was highly vulnerable, needing adventure to understand how to maneuver properly in an East Asian country as a young American, unable to connect through deep conversations.

Through this highly vulnerable position I was placed in, I was pushed to grow my comprehension of Asian body language, the Mandarin language, and the culture around me while figuring out how I wanted to live day by day. Being alone pushed me to be independent and a self-starter. Naturally, I grew more through this isolation, discovering how to operate in the unknown as time passed.

Looking back on my life, I have realized that in moments where I knew the least were some of the best of my life. For example, flying to India without a phone for fifteen days was extraordinary at seventeen. I had never been outside of the United States until that moment, and being able to experience a different culture while not knowing a lot about it was a moment I will never forget—the street monkeys and cows, the abnormally dangerous nonstop rush-hour traffic, and the delicious, do-not-eat-with-your-left hand food. This trip remained vividly in my brain for a few years because of its profound impact on me to open up like never before and find a way to relate to a different culture while curating a new daily routine. I realized I loved traveling because it forced me to be uncomfortable. I think this discomfort is essential for vulnerability, and vulnerability is paramount for growth. The trick is to be comfortable with discomfort. Hence, evolution is supremely natural and continuous without extreme force or unnecessary pain.

Everything in the world only grows when it can be vulnerable. In his 2019 speech, "Why We Get Sick," for the How To Academy's presentation titled "Dr. Gabor Maté on the Connection between Stress and Disease," Doctor Maté explains that we, as human beings, have two fundamental needs in our life: authenticity and attachment. Put simply, when these seemingly basic needs are unmet, we get sick (Maté 2019).

A lot of us play roles in our lives to please others. This perpetual role-playing is stress-inducing. This role-playing also gets in the way of forming genuine connections and real attachments. A person stuck in this role-playing cycle is killing two birds, needs, with one stone—a faulty lifestyle.

On his brilliant October 2022 appearance on the Jay Shetty podcast, Doctor Maté explained that a sense of purpose could only arise when we are in touch with our true selves. So while stuck in this chameleon state, we are hindering our basic needs while also disengaging from what God put us here to do (Shetty 2022).

This vulnerability sprouts from being honest with yourself and your emotions and actions. An essential piece to the puzzle is not to suppress your feelings but to let them live and acknowledge them for what they are: real, raw, and intentional. Listen to your feelings and thoughts to unlock what your heart is feeding you. This compassionate listening will enable one to live intrinsically rather than extrinsically, balanced by the self rather than the wind of the outside world.

A 2019 article by Excelsior University by Elaine Bontempi explains the motivation and the energy that pushes us to behave the way we do. Intrinsic motivation comes from sincere interest, while extrinsic motivation comes from extrinsic rewards. Furthermore, intrinsic motivation usually creates creativity, passion, and enthusiasm—characteristics synonymous with excellence in any field (Bontempi 2019).

According to the theory of motivation, people have three crucial needs: relatedness, competence, and autonomy. These three needs are met more easily when the working environment is looser with far fewer demands and rules, so employees can have independence while being able to adapt and relate to those they find can help them master work concepts (Bontempi 2019).

Rather than focusing strictly on pay or benefits, as a working person, it is important to focus on the work environment to decipher whether the conditions will allow you to be vulnerable and grow. An environment that promotes working intrinsically rather than strictly for company rewards will allow you to be yourself and explore your skills as they relate to the role. Living aloud passionately will allow you to thrive and fully realize who you are while maintaining a sense of balance—centered within your desires and not those of the people around you (Bontempi 2019).

Why, as human beings, do we find it so hard to be ourselves? Because we care so much about the emotional needs of others. Their opinions. Their wants. Their validation of our actions. This unconditional care drives many people to forget about their own needs. So while society may encourage us to be unique, in America, I see packs of individuals in tribes acting as a unit for a sense of belonging. Maté explains in his 2019 speech to the How To Academy that even obituaries illustrate that what we value in others is what kills them—outwork yourself. He also explains that people believe two major misconceptions:

1. You are responsible for how other people feel.

2. You should always satisfy everyone (Maté 2019).

Both of these beliefs are hugely incorrect. First, being compulsively driven to help others because you want them to love you is a significant problem. Second, when we repress emotions to make others feel more comfortable, we experience all the other emotions on the spectrum less. The key to unlocking a beautiful, stress-free life is self-awareness and compassion. This genuine love for yourself and others may help reverse childhood pain, trauma, and depression.

Jack Kornfield, the author of *The Wise Heart*, explains this self-awareness as nonjudgmental with loving awareness. Kornfield trained as a Buddhist Monk in Thailand, Burma, and India, where he learned what applying "mindful attention" truly means. In his talk "Jack Kornfield: The Ancient Heart of Forgiveness" for the Greater Good Science Center in 2011, he explains that we must learn to grieve and let go consistently. We must fully experience feelings of bargaining, loss, fear, and anger while truly embracing these emotions, allowing them to "season" who we are as we grow with it (Greater Good Science Center 2011).

Kornfield mentions that forgiveness includes all dimensions of our life, including our mind and body. Therefore, we must learn to process and understand our inner feelings and emotions to grow our capacity for trustworthy awareness. He references a quote by a fellow author and friend, Anne Lamott:

"My mind is like a bad neighborhood. I try to not go there alone" (Greater Good Science Center 2011).

Lamott humorously references the frightening phenomenon that Kornfield explains further. Our mind goes in circles with few new thoughts each day. It is hard to lose thoughts, especially toxic ones that may make us feel guilty, stressed, or worried. Being grounded and mindful, especially in the Buddhist context that Kornfield trained in, can allow one to abandon evil thoughts or even replace bad thoughts to move on successfully (Greater Good Science Center 2011).

In his talk at the Stanford Memorial Church on November 10, 2015, during Stanford's "Contemplation by Design Week," Kornfield explains that as we train our heart, body, and mind, we begin to live with our loneliness better. This comfortable livelihood is possible because most of the issues with our inner experience do not come from our inner experience but rather our constant resistance. We must fully accept each feeling we have while labeling them for what they are. Through loving acceptance and awareness, one can embrace their undying spirit through love no matter how the world treats them. Finding gratitude and self-love is more manageable when one understands that everyone experiences pain, as it is synonymous with the human condition. On a more philosophical note, Kornfield states about mindfulness and interconnectedness:

"The question is not the future of humanity, but the presence of eternity" (Stanford University 2015).

The key to embracing this presence and getting over the past is to utilize mindful intention, breathing life, love, and compassion into our daily actions in the present day.

A MEDITATIVE STRESS-FREE LIFE

The movie *Office Space* (1999) is a beautiful example of decluttering your life and reducing stress to become more successful. The main character gets hypnotized to be in a consistent state of relaxation. Some would call it a state of meditation, where everything is "Zen." When this shift happens, everything in his life starts to shape up: his love life, work life, and overall personal well-being. He is the epitome of the phrase: "Just Be."

A great dichotomy between relaxed and excited needs to be acknowledged. Some people are in a consistent low-energy expression as if nothing matters. This expression is great as a baseline, but it is also important to experience life's joyful moments and have positive arousal. So while it is important to stay level-headed and poised, it is also essential to be happy, laugh, love, and fully experience life's spectrum of emotions.

I suppose the dichotomy is while experiencing life's many chaotic moments, knowing that each moment becomes new and that feeling needs to return as soon as possible. The yin is that moment experienced fully, and the yang is the ability to move to the next as if that moment never happened: ready, prepared, and unfazed. To keep going, we must continue finding what excites us and utilize this passion in compelling and creative ways that fulfill our being. This cycle is why intrinsically living can help us overcome pits of darkness or stagnation. Peter A Levine, PhD and author of *Waking the Tiger: Healing Trauma*, explains this beautifully for his Ergos Institute of Somatic Education:

> "The body has been designed to renew itself through continuous self-correction. These same principles also apply to the healing of psyche, spirit, and soul" (Levine 2022).

I was speaking to Bawa Jain, the president and founder of The Centre for Leadership. We agreed that meditation is not an act. Instead, it is a state of being. Jain, who has spent time with Muammar Gaddafi and Nelson Mandela, declared, "Meditation is a state where your mind is thoughtless: the thoughts are speechless, the body is lifeless, and you are in absolute relaxation. Your inner being is in equanimity, balanced, and still."

In other words, you are not attached to anything while going about your daily life. Jain and I agree that one's goal should be to be in this state of being for every moment, charging yourself up.

Simplicity is key. I often live an action-oriented and straight-forward life: wake, act, impact, repeat. This mentality of simplicity arises from living intrinsically and doing what feels right within each moment: making my morning oatmeal, watching the news, scootering to school, listening to a playlist, playing with my students, and doing my best to connect deeper with each person throughout the day. I stay off social media and focus on whatever I can control throughout my day. Refraining from overthinking breeds itself to exploration and the ability to impact people along the way selflessly. Simplifying complex ideas leads to peace. In your mind, there will never be absolute peace as there will always be difficult moments when darkness creeps in or hard times come. However, you can control how long you stay in each state of mind and how much focus you place on gratitude and mindfulness.

Meditating is vital because it allows one to feel in control of their lives while feeling an essential sense of ease with who they are, what they want, and where they are going in their lives. Meditation allows one to ease any psychological or physical tension they may be experiencing by allowing them to let go completely. Letting go releases any pent-up worrying by bringing about what Kornfield describes as "loving awareness."

Meditation can be performed in many different ways. In my life, I pray in the morning when I wake up, asking God for guidance and reassurance that I remain calm, collected, and in a state of pure gratitude, expecting and assuming nothing. I use apps called Calm and Inspirations to stay meditative throughout the day while also connecting with the Bible, my spiritual text. Phone applications can be beneficial because they provide music and spoken word that can guide mindfulness meditations. Some other mindfulness apps include Headspace, Breethe, and Buddhify.

Additionally, meditation bowls can be extremely helpful in getting into a relaxed setting. The sound rings and echoes until complete silence as you keep your eyes closed. My religion teachers at my Catholic high school used these bowls, which were highly effective in helping to calm everyone.

Ultimately, developing a mindfulness routine aims to heal from trauma and release any pent-up worrying lingering within the mind that can cause unnecessary stress. The goal of living a relaxed life is to allow us to let down our guard, be ourselves, and not be swayed by public opinion. When doing this, we must remember the need to play specific roles in each situation, which is the most significant factor in creating unneeded stress. Connecting to our inner self and inner being allows us to forget about unnatural expectations and live genuinely and authentically within ourselves. So stop worrying because everything will always be okay. Calm down and do your best; everything will work out without force. Worrying worsens the circumstances and perpetuates stress driven by anxiety and self-imposed walls created to divide or hide from yourself and the public.

CHAPTER 18

Empathetic Leadership: Learn to Listen

"Leadership is about empathy. It is about having the ability to relate to and connect with people for the purpose of inspiring and empowering their lives."
—OPRAH WINFREY

On November 2, I was in my office on the first floor of Peng Nan Junior High, watching the clouds circle the sky as another typhoon began to hit the islands of Penghu. Scootering becomes dangerous, biking becomes impossible, playing sports outside becomes unappealing, and people stay inside mostly away from the patchy, sling-shotted rain, watching movies and curling up with a blanket. The unpredictable windiness and storm are like leadership—dealing with unexpected twists, turns, and outbursts while attempting to remain calm, collected, and reasonable. I was gearing up for an interview with Bawa Jain, very well-accomplished in the religious world and the founder of The Centre for Responsible Leadership.

I have mentioned Jain before, but his leadership career is prominent and intriguing. Jain founded The Centre for Responsible Leadership, whose main job is to create a world where all leaders from different walks of life, business sectors, and economic backgrounds can reflect on their role as responsible leaders, creating the future for the next generation. I respect that the group is "nonpartisan, inclusive, and collaborative," seeking to bring together diverse minds effectively. Jain was a secretary of the Millennium Summit of the United Nations after working in the corporate world for a while. Jain says the most excellent untapped resource in the world is religious leaders. I agree with him. You do not often come across a company, school, or businessman with religion in the back of his mind. Jain, a meditator like me, founded The Centre for Responsible Leadership to harness religious leaders.

Trust is huge, and Jain believes religious leaders are natural givers, seeking to unite through awareness and being fully conscious.

When was the last time a leader asked you about your awareness of your mind, body, and soul? These components are the essence of spirituality—being honest with yourself and others. Did you come into a space to exploit or to give? A leader should be coming into spaces to provide and to understand, not to figure out avenues for exploitation. Jain has met many empathetic and compassionate leaders while also being empowered.

Jain says Nelson Mandela had this innate ability to make others feel comfortable with themselves because of his humility and trustworthiness under his larger-than-life image. The United States still had his face on the terrorist list at the time, and he did not care.

A great example of an empathetic leader who balanced compassion and fought well is Nelson Mandela. Mandela was a militant commander trying to seek freedom from South Africa. He spent twenty-seven years in prison simply for wanting to seek out peace. When he was released, he treated his time in prison as a minor blip in his monumental life: "As I was saying the other day…"

A great leader is a great listener. Live your truth and have conviction. However, respect everyone's differing opinions. A great leader realizes this dichotomy of utilizing his platform while placing others on this platform as well. They know mutual respect and how to listen to words and body language. Leaders surrender to the moment because they understand that life unfolds naturally, and force or anger will only hurt the situation.

During his time working with the United Nations as a secretary of the Millennium Summit, Jain also met Muammar Gaddafi—brotherly leader and guide of the Revolution of Libya—in a tent, which was his usual place of casual meetups, to discuss interrelations between the UN and Libya. Gaddafi was angry at the UN for not meeting his expectations for Libya during this particular meeting. However, during the meeting with the UN, he patiently waited and listened to everything the secretary said, even though he pissed him off. This empathetic listening paid dividends to the rest of Gaddafi's reign, resolving the argument and lessening Gaddafi's heightened emotions.

Jain had a similar experience when being torn apart by a colleague in the UN. Similar to his experience with Gaddafi, Jain again listened and paid respect with integrity. He sincerely took in every word even though he was being torn apart angrily. Jain's listening created peace rather than war. Because of his ability to stay poised and calm, the argument was resolved quickly, bringing harmony to the conflict.

A LEADER'S MIND-SET: ALL-IN MENTALITY

I was approaching another Friday music release day in Taiwan. All music is released at midnight American Eastern Time on Friday. Back in the states, I was usually excited to listen to new tracks every Thursday night. As I scrolled through YouTube, watching artist interviews with Zane Lowe on Apple Music or The Breakfast Club Power 105, I came across an interview with Derek Jeter and Angie Martinez.

I have always been drawn to interviews because I like deciphering the mind-sets of great performers, athletes, and artists. Jeter, one of the best shortstops of all time in Major League Baseball and a hall of famer, sat down with Angie Martinez, radio hall of famer, in October 2022 on her IRL

Podcast. IRL stands for "in real life." The acronym has become quite popular in the hyphenated texting language of today's American culture.

Similar to interviews with athletic greats like Kobe and Lebron, Jeter was no different: calm, honest, and humble. "The last thing you think is the first thing you do," Jeter declares. One hundred percent. When in a relaxed mental state, there exists no doubt or overthinking of the past or the future. You exist as a being in the world, allowing your passions and interests to carry you to the following obligation (Martinez 2022).

As a leader, understanding that greatness is never a goal, but simply having a consistent mind-set allows one to enjoy the process while having no expectations and no assumptions. Like a professional athlete or a film director, when you are passionate about something, the motivation to always want to do it will never leave. Like the trump card in a game of bridge or pinochle—my grandparents' favorite games—living for the process trumps all other intentions. The end goal is simply a side effect or a great reward from hard work, listening, or learning.

Time in life is precious. I was speaking to Randall Nadeau, the executive director of the Foundation for Scholarly Exchange for Fulbright Taiwan. We were eating at Apatite restaurant in the Four Points Sheraton in Penghu. This night was after a beautiful conference to bring together Fulbright officials and the mayor to celebrate Fulbright and spotlight renewable energy and sustainability projects in the area. I remember meeting local Taiwanese and Fulbright officials from the United States. All the officials were incredibly warm and gracious, fully committed to supporting our needs and asking us several questions about our likings, wants, and concerns. The officials were in tune with all the students and attendees—truly listening intently with care.

Nadeau told me that the most crucial action for me to take while I am in Taiwan is simply taking it in. Be a sponge. Listen to others while finding time to immerse myself in the culture. I recognize that several people enter into phases of their lives with expectations and clear outlines. I know now, however, that a leader can be so powerful because they lose themselves in the people they are leading.

For instance, while eating in Apatite with Doctor Nadeau, we sat with my roommate and other Fulbrighters nearby to discuss his background and connect with each of us. What wowed me were his individualized questions. He wanted to know who we were, what we wanted to get out of Fulbright, and what we wanted to do with the rest of our careers. He listened intently to our stories and responded in ways he could help. It was genuinely incredible seeing him lose himself in all of us as if we were his purpose and his lifetime, giving his energy to us thoroughly and comprehensively. In this way, by letting down his guard, he allowed everyone sitting at the table to open up. This unwinding demonstrates the importance of vulnerability to empower others to be vulnerable and enhance the connection between everyone.

After the Christmas holiday and a visit to Butterfly Cafe for Italian food and laughs with some of my friends, I talked to

Doctor Nadeau over Zoom from my apartment in downtown Magong.

I welcomed him into my virtual room and told him about my busy Thursday teaching at Peng Nan Junior High and Wude Elementary across the street. After I told him about my exploration of the yin-yang symbol, Nadeau muttered, "There cannot be any reality without both yin and yang. The original meaning of yin yang is breathing in and out."

I sat back in my chair and smiled. I replied, "Exactly. A combination of receptiveness and expressiveness and finding a way to harness the balance between both, so they both can thrive while you thrive."

I asked, "I am curious how you listen when you lead. How do you carry both yin and yang effectively as you communicate with Fulbright officials?"

He said, "There is definitely a complementary relationship between leaders and followers. My leadership philosophy is to empower my staff to act and make decisions. I do not give the staff the illusion, but the reality of agency."

We discussed the importance of inclusivity and the definition of diversity, equity, and inclusion (DEI) in Taiwan, which features a largely homogeneous society as opposed to America. For Nadeau, it is about allowing teachers to dictate how they teach, similar to how students dictate how they want to learn. This sentiment is very accurate, as we have started to evolve our curriculum in my school to focus more on project-based learning. Our discussion progressed to the power of yoga and meditation in leadership. Yoga at its core comes from the Sanskrit root "yoke," which often means "control," according to Nadeau. This "control" involves many disciplines, and leadership and discipline go hand-in-hand. Without discipline, leaders could not effectively lead while leveraging listening and directing.

Near the end of our fruitful discussion, I exclaimed, "As a leader, I think to prosper within this special discipline, we must develop a specific mindfulness routine where we can center ourselves consistently, so we do not get upset from negativity and pressure."

Nadeau replied, "We often get into situations where unwelcome thoughts control us rather than us controlling them. The trick is to harness our thoughts rather than allowing our thoughts to harness us."

Meditation allows one to let go of ego to look at life as objects of consciousness rather than rigid pieces of who you are. This grounding enables a leader to forget about their own needs to comfort the needs of their students through genuine listening.

While teaching, I want to make my students feel comfortable and heard at all times. I want them to understand that my engagement is not for me. Still, whenever they need help or more guidance, I am there to ensure they can reach a place of stability and comfort while learning. It is not about me, and it is never about me. It is about losing myself in my students. Any empathetic leader loses himself in everyone else, empowering and encouraging by humbly being present.

The dichotomy attempts to make your presence known while empowering others to do the same in every moment of your life.

MINDFUL AND VULNERABLE LEADERSHIP

Jennifer A. Hill, CEO and founder of Optimal Match, describes her leadership style as embodying what she wants to teach.

She explains, "When I am reactive as a leader, I lose credibility in the eyes of those I am leading, as it is out of integrity with whom I am claiming to be. To be a great leader, I believe it is important to show up in a clean and authentic way every day."

Hill recalls when one of her employees felt rejected and unappreciated because she was processing an extremely complex payroll. Using her intuition, Hill noticed something was wrong, so she privately apologized, which brought the employee to tears and single-handedly saved them from quitting. Another habit Hill practices is asking herself or someone close to her whether she has caused anyone pain today.

Hill and I both agree that this unashamed curiosity and honesty with oneself is a beautiful leadership technique that could develop brilliant leaders and human beings.

Brené Brown's Dare to Lead Hub states, "A leader is anyone who takes responsibility for finding the potential in people and processes and has courage to develop that potential" (Brown 2023).

Brown's leadership philosophy is centered on the heart, not being afraid of vulnerability but leaning into the emotions and all the difficult conversations that rightfully come with it. In my leadership cohort in college, we often called leadership the willingness to step into the "void" where no one usually dares to step (Brown 2023).

This definition intersects with Brown's sentiment that leadership takes courage, self-awareness, and the ability to be unafraid amid potential failure. If we do not know who we are, how can we help others? That is why finding balance through intentional centeredness and purposeful mindfulness is essential to perpetuate a healthy sense of self as an example to others. A listening ear means nothing when the listening end is lost within their minds, constantly distracted by their shortcomings, wants, or needs. One must be secure with themselves, so their courageousness can rub off on everyone else in the room while the sharer feels heard, valued, and respected.

I had the excellent opportunity to speak to Mary Mackey, an influential professor, novelist, poet, screenwriter, and scholar. Mackey earned a BA from Harvard College and a PhD in Comparative Literature from the University of Michigan. She has authored eight collections of poetry and fourteen novels, many of which have made the *New York Times* and *San Francisco Chronicle* bestseller lists. Interestingly, empathy has been a huge helping factor in her career. Mackey credits her Harvard Professor Richard Evans Schultes, famous American botanist, with helping her unlock peace through nature and being silent with herself. She expresses that silence allows humans to travel deep inside themselves, uncovering that inner space is connected to all outer space. This connection helped her foster empathy.

Speaking about her students, Mackey acknowledges that impact can only grow from empathy. Inspiration sprouts from seeing and understanding her students. Mackey states, "Empathy is the glue that allows the world to go round…the clue to successful mentorship." Back when Mackey was teaching every semester, she had several more minor creative writing courses, where she had individual interviews—almost colleague to colleague in some ways.

It is precious for her students to have personal contact. A genuine and deep academic or work-related connection is invaluable to a successful career and happiness. Interestingly, almost no one ever decided what they wanted to do without meeting someone they admired within that same field. Empathy allows us to understand who we want to be and why by enabling us to put ourselves in the shoes of others and ultimately connect with those people by learning or teaching.

Listen to your heart. Listen to your deepest desires. Then, most importantly, listen to the people who count on you because empathetic leadership is one of the world's highest quality and underrated forms of leadership. There is no better feeling than meeting someone who understands or tries to understand you. Be that someone and it will pay off in the end.

CHAPTER 19

An *Often*-Unmatched Symbiotic Pair: Business and Spirituality

---

"Business is a spiritual game. As a business owner or entrepreneur, it is your opportunity to do more for others than anybody else—in whatever area or industry you're in."
—TONY ROBBINS

A few weeks after Chinese New Year and celebrating 2023's Year of the Rabbit festivities, I visited Sun Moon Lake in the foothills of Taiwan's Central Mountain range. The lake in Yuchi Township, Nantou County, Taiwan, is the largest body of water in the country. Tasting moments of spring in the air as the sun began to take over the cold winter of Taiwan, I took in the beautiful scenery of the green mountains. I noticed several people visiting at the same time as me, and I immediately realized this place was a tourist sanctuary. It was peaceful and gorgeous and full of business: sales merchants on the streets, boats driving people across the lake hourly, and hotels along the lake. This relationship between peace and fast-paced competition, calmness and chaos, and nature and tourism made me ponder the relationship between business and spirituality.

Can businesses thrive when they are centered in a clear sense of purpose and grounding? Can a true sense of religion and understanding that there is a higher power than us compel us to perform our day-to-day objectives with a truer form of mindfulness, intention, and attitude? I think so.

It was the first day of February. I woke up, enjoyed my morning coffee, and then got on a call with Mona Sobhani, author of *Proof of Spiritual Phenomena: A Neuroscientist's Discovery of the Ineffable Mysteries of the Universe* and founder and CEO of Conscious Cognition Consulting.

I wanted to explore this idea of business and spirituality with Mona. Mona had just begun reading *The Myth of Normal* by Gabor Maté and felt that trauma and corporate culture are not set up for humanity and nature. She states, "Everything is not set up to support us."

Spirituality is the meaning you make of life. Whatever system of beliefs you prescribe. Our interactions have much meaning. This meaning is tied into how you make meaning of yourself and your intention as you move through life.

Mona believes spirituality should be more critical than it is: "American business has no room for humanity. The purpose of business is to increase profits, which comes at the cost of our humanity."

Especially when it comes to business and making money, she and I both agree that infusing spiritual intentions and consciousness into our culture is paramount. Today, the benefit corporation and social purpose corporations exist, which both aim to perform specific socially conscious activities that nonprofits often focus on.

When business owners balance their time and ground themselves, they begin to get rid of unneeded stress and intensity to better complete their job without losing their personal happiness or satisfaction. This grounding comes with centeredness, calmness, and a meditative state of mind—qualities present in any spiritual undertaking, regardless of religion.

Mona admits that without a mindfulness routine, she had anxious energy. She was hearing things, and she was not fully present. Now, with a straightforward mindfulness routine and a steady grip on meditation, she powerfully relates to the people she works with, opening up space to see, hear, and understand them. She actively brings herself to the moment and stays tuned to her body.

What is possible with a clear mind is boundless and limitless. When spirituality becomes a vital component of business, Mona and I strongly concur that efficiency blossoms in the form of a calm, centered, and grounded flower watered consistently—growing steadily and peacefully in a field of many flowers while relating to them all. Developing this precise peace of mind and unbothered nature as a flower may take a while. Still, it works wonders, as spirituality is a priority in the working world. Comparison and competition do not matter as much because a spiritual leader focuses on personal and group development, joyful abundance, and genuine connectivity.

THE NEW TYPE OF LEADER IS A SPIRITUAL LEADER

Martin Olando, principal at Anglican Church of Kenya (ACK) Bishop Hannington Institute of Theology and Development, believes that spirituality breeds robust business. He states, "Spirituality influences how one carries out business. In most cases, one who is spiritual will carry out business with integrity." Spirituality often allows us to let go of our force and allow life to unfold as it should. Olando, like me, is a Christian. This faith, which encourages patience, a nonjudgmental attitude, forgiveness, and letting bitterness go, has enabled Olando to lead with mindfulness.

Olando acknowledges, "I use mindfulness in my leadership by being tolerant, being patient with people, and striving to serve everyone fairly. This gives me inner peace and satisfaction. I have also developed trust in myself and my instincts."

Olando and I agreed on one fundamental idea: Spirituality influences how we value ourselves, allowing us to grow our self-esteem. Furthermore, spiritual people may believe they are made in God's image. Olando continues, "The fact that I have God's image of creativity and ability to think ensures I make balanced decisions."

Olando makes a great point here; the deep grounding from becoming spiritual enables one to detach from the physical world and turn inward to find true confidence from within. When we feel secure with who we are and what we offer the world, we stop feeling so anxious about our decisions as we truly understand God has our back unconditionally with support and forgiveness. Balance is easier to maintain in a tranquil state of mind that is not distracted or pushed to anger and stress easily.

Think of working for a boss who has a calming and caring presence. This boss enables a business to be performed efficiently and powerfully, as it should be. The workflow in the office is natural, flowing as the black and white sides of the yin-yang symbol flow into each other. Nothing is forced; instead, everything happens when it is supposed to, in the right amount of time and at the right pace.

According to a 2019 *Frontiers in Psychology* article by researchers at Henan University and the University of Waikato, spiritual leadership has three main components: vision, hope, and altruistic love. Vision entails discovering a deeply meaningful future, which in turn inspires intrinsic value and living intentionally. Hope entails the leader's genuine confidence in achieving the vision. Altruistic love entails specific leadership behaviors that bring about care, respect, and understanding (Wang et al. 2019).

This type of leadership is invaluable to any organization trying to maintain loyal and hardworking employees while pushing the envelope in innovation. Without a genuine connection and acknowledging the presence of something bigger beyond you, a business can become tiresome and bland, losing purpose.

The *Forbes* article "What Does It Mean to Be a Spiritual Leader in the Workplace?" explains that 75 percent of Americans label themselves as spiritual. In comparison, 28 percent of Americans have credited the pandemic for deepening their faith (Byrnes 2022).

When it comes to incorporating a sense of spirituality within leadership, *Forbes* author Kelly Byrnes explains it: "Think of spiritual leadership as creating an environment of trust, honor and success for all. Keep it simple, reasonable and responsible" (Byrnes 2022).

I like this description by Byrnes because it describes maintaining a positive environment for all while remaining realistic and keeping low expectations. An essential quality of a spiritual leader is maintaining a level sense of humbleness and grounding, allowing employees' real humanity to shine through such accurate decisions that can be made rather than greedy decisions.

This free environment reminds me a lot of the working environment at Netflix, headquartered in my hometown of Los Gatos, California. With the classic phrase "No Rules Rules," Reed Hastings, the cofounder and executive chairman of Netflix, has developed a working environment to trust in teamwork, always be honest, and never get into the habit of pleasing your boss. The environment truly welcomes flexibility, wellness, and innovation rather than pure speed. The lack of stress and constraints allows employees to have autonomy and dictate their working patterns and pace to fit their deepest feelings and needs. This autonomy enables self-care and reflection—two components essential to develop a sense of powerful spirituality (Hastings and Meyer, 2020).

Spirituality has a solid and firm foundation within the service of others. Reed Hastings experienced a life of service before becoming the billionaire and famous American entrepreneur he is today. According to *Encyclopedia Britannica*, Hastings served in the US Marine Corps after graduating from Bowdoin College and spent two years in the Peace Corps, teaching math in Swaziland. Undoubtedly, this experience of committed service in his life prepared him well to lead a company redefining the workplace environment. He cares about his well-being and the well-being of all his employees, and it has paid off huge dividends. Creating a company with a foundation of service, grounding, and heart will build a prosperous situation. In Netflix's case, it did tenfold (Hibler 2023).

A MINDFUL BUSINESS LEADER: SURRENDER TO GRATITUDE
Speaking with Renee Blodgett, founder of Blue Soul Earth and editor of We Blog the World, we nudged toward the precise reason that business and spirituality coexist in beautiful harmony—high-quality and careful leadership. Blodgett states:

> Mindfulness in your daily life isn't separate from mindfulness in your leadership. Just as consciousness is pervasive, mindfulness is too, for when it is integral to who

you are, it changes everything and everyone around you. When mindfulness *becomes you*, you are conscious of how you act, the words you say, who you spend your time with, and the decisions you make, in every moment of your day.

Business leaders must ask themselves essential questions to guide their steps in the world. What is the fundamental source of my decisions? Fear or love? Are my choices made with the whole team in mind or simply a few people? Blodgett continues on leadership: "Heart-centered living is at the core, and this starts in your personal life, which naturally extends to your professional one. If it's who you are, then there are no borders between who you are at home and who you are in the boardroom."

As I sit in my room at the Crystal Hotel Taipei, looking out into an overcast and cloudy Taiwanese sky, I cannot help but think that life is so often what we make of it and how we perceive every moment. I could use the day how I please, whether outside my comfort zone or inside it. I consistently choose outside, walking an hour to Longshan Riverside Park. Gratitude drives my steps and purpose and allows me to take steps with a smile.

Like a successful person, a successful business needs a purpose to thrive. This purpose is derived from mindfulness, awareness, and attention to feelings, surroundings, and needs. A spiritual person walks into their purpose without hesitation or fear. Lao Tzu, the founder of Taoism, says:

"To the mind that is still, the whole universe surrenders" (TCM World 2020).

If business leaders want doors to open up, they must surrender to reality and what is in store. Answers are often right
in front of you. All a leader must do is look down, take it in,
and be highly attentive and appreciative of what has been
built already.

Spirituality allows us to see each other in a new way and a
new light—optimistically, truthfully, and thoroughly. As chi
represents the interconnected energy force within Taoism
or Daoism, a spiritual leader can embrace this and see the
interconnectedness of their business. Although it may be
somewhat mystical, this force is vibrant. It mirrors the interconnectedness of the yin-yang symbol, representing a beautiful connective tissue that lasts forever and is omnipresent.
A business leader who can acknowledge this interconnected
tissue within their business will garner more natural success
and opportunity.

I discussed the critical intersection of business and spirituality with Paul Coutinho. Coutinho is the author of *How
Big Is Your God?: The Freedom to Experience the Divine* and
an internationally recognized scholar and speaker blending
spirituality and psychology. Paul explains, "One of the goals
of spirituality is to find the meaning and message of our lives.
In business, we must find ways of living out our personal
meaning and message."

Put in this way, it is easier to comprehend that our spirituality directly informs or should inform our business decisions because our businesses reflect who we are and what we want to bring into the world. When grounded in the meaning of who exactly we are, our companies should run more smoothly, efficiently, and authentically.

Coutinho and I agree that the goal of spirituality is to answer the existential questions of life: Who am I? What is my true purpose in this life?

No matter what religion, a spiritual person can agree on one thing: All human beings are divine. The scriptures of all religions point to human beings being divine. Coutinho, a professor of psychology and organizational studies at Saint Louis University and Lindenwood University, shares that he finds his essence in the second chapter of the *Book of Genesis*. In this chapter, God takes dust, forms it into the shape of man, breathes his breath into it, and the man becomes a living being. Coutinho reminds himself that he is the divine breath, so he finds peace when focused on breathing. This presence, called the "I-NOW-HERE," allows him to be a better teacher.

Business leaders should always recognize the brilliance in front of them and feel a sense of gratitude for their employees. A business leader fully immersed in the present moment but detached from the selfish ego emotionally is critical for sustained success. Whereas a heavy connection to ego blocks us from truly connecting to others, practicing humility and detaching from the continuous need for personal gains to be genuinely present at the moment allows us to create lasting and profound relationships. These relationships thrive because they feed our souls rather than our ego due to a mental state that embraces independence, growth, and positivity. When one embraces authentic immersion wholeheartedly, they become neutral to their emotions while being able to act from a grounded and centered place. This mind state is easier to achieve once spirituality is unlocked. It starts with small victories like meditating for a few minutes or finding time to pray. Coutinho says,

> "When we go to bed with gratitude, again, the subconscious and the unconscious will continue looking for things to be grateful for."

Go to bed with gratitude. Find reasons to keep waking up excited to take on the day, and spend time with people who are eager to work on the same vision you have. Business and spirituality are an unmatched symbiotic pair destined for greatness and powerful enough to withstand adversity.

BALANCE IN LEADERSHIP

Alex Moses, founder of Stairway to Success, is a business developer with a foundation in Taoism. He has worked with the likes of Steve Jobs and Paul Allen. His approach combines human behavior and business strategy with spiritual insights to help his clients generate revenue efficiently. After connecting with Moses, we had much to digest on this fascinating and relevant pair. Moses exclaims:

"Mindfulness is the bridge that connects a leader's mind to the hearts of their employees and the soul of the business."

I like to think a spiritual leader is a multi-dimensional leader, willing to go the extra mile to truly understand what lies underneath feelings: employees' intentions, customers' wants, and stockholders' desires. Moses and I agree that spirituality manifests itself in business when those involved clearly balance personal and professional fulfillment.

A spiritual leader operates from the heart—from a place of warmth, not from a cold place of exploitation and greed. When leaders genuinely balance themselves emotionally, it is difficult for any adversary or competitor to knock them off their feet or rile them up. When anger is nonexistent and stress no longer overwhelms but informs graciously, a leader is an anchor that grounds, uplifts, and calms.

Speaking with renowned TEDx Speaker Janet Nambi about her experience as a burnout prevention coach and being the CEO and founder of Unconscious Brilliance, I further understood the place of spirituality as a root of business. Nambi is Islamic, and her mindfulness practice has allowed her to use self-love to create the boundaries she needs to foster balance. In her experience as a coach, Nambi utilizes meditation and written tools such as self-compassion, practicing acceptance, releasing self-judgment, and creating boundaries to help her clients reattach to their authentic spirits, harnessing self-love.

Nambi can impact people positively because of her spirituality. When I asked her about the intersection between leadership and spirituality, Nambi used a powerful word encompassing the nature of many great leaders—openness. Openness breeds a broader perspective and fundamental, genuine belief in others. Nambi reasons well: "Spiritual leaders also base a lot of their decision-making on their moral authority, which allows for more humanness. For these reasons, spiritual leaders connect easily with their followers and therefore are able to speak to both the heart and mind to increase impact."

I spoke with Adam Hergenrother, founder of Livian and author of *The 200% Life* and *The Founder & The Force Multiplier,* about the vital pairing of business and spirituality. Hergenrother believes that a company and spirituality *must* coexist rather than *should* coexist. Hergenrother likes to think of "spiritual leadership" as conscious leadership. He teaches his team this concept daily—awareness, using the mind as a tool, and the ability to remain poised in stressful situations.

Hergenrother acknowledges that some business professionals may perceive spirituality as "too soft," driving some to fall off and lose their competitive edge. However, the advantages far outweigh the disadvantages. Balance and peace win any day over stress and toxic win-at-all-costs behavior. When business and spiritual awakening collide, Hergenrother declares, "We get companies that are just as conscious of humanity, the environment, and the world as they are about growth and profit. We get businesspeople who can communicate with honesty, transparency, and vulnerability in order to get shit done without becoming attached to the outcome. We get a whole ecosystem of people who are clear, centered, and neutral, who make decisions from this place of clarity." When the conscious is controlled, genuine joy, enthusiasm, and creativity permeate like a virtuous wildfire.

Balance in leadership with dark emotions (yin) and intense action (yang) can be achieved via spiritual practices such as meditation, mindfulness, yoga, prayer, and fellowship. Yin is stillness and the ultimate void where creation exists, while yang is the spark. Yang is most successful after periods of stillness. Stillness before action is a meditation into mindfulness at its best.

Halloween at Doors Cafe

Fulbright Award Ceremony

Gelato Shop with Leo

Guanyintingguoji Coast Park

High Five Completed

High Five after Chinese Checkers

In Milksha (Magong, Penghu)

Hot Pot

Jersey Tag with students

Peng Nan Junior High Soccer Field

Peng Nan Junior High Entrance

Peng Nan Junior High Faculty Photo

Principe Restaurant in Tainan

Penghu Recreation Area

Scuba Diving near Shanshui Fishing Pier

Pescadores Resort (occasional lunch and dinner spot)

Stir Fry Restaurant

Pescadores Resort for Taiwanese Dinner

Teaching about India

Teaching about New York Bagels

Teaching about Sri Lanka

Teaching Goodbye

The Danish Republic

The Eatery with co-teacher Leo

Conclusion

Most of us do not realize that the most crucial resource of our lives is time. We can never get back time that is lost. We can earn money and try to rekindle a friendship, but we can never go back in time.

Recently, after becoming a minimalist and giving away several of my clothes to Goodwill while becoming interested in community service and teaching, I have come to understand that my life is filled with beauty and wonder when I strive to connect, learn, and grow. I am never content with breezing through life, unchanged or unconscious, to what I can achieve with what is in front of me. The beauty before you is truly endless when tapped into its true potential. But what is in front of you is also all you have, so make the most of it.

In a 2022 video by Better Ideas titled "Your life was already decided," narrator Joey Schweitzer mentions a simple yet profound statement: "Whether you thought about today or not, you still got here…all of the pain of overcoming mental resistance so that you could do things that are beneficial to you and all the pleasure of comfort that you engaged in by playing Overwatch 2 and eating takeout. It's all gone now… All you have is the result of those past ninety days, so what do you have to show for it" (Schweitzer 2022). It's a beautiful sentiment explaining that time is precious and vital. Time possesses the ability to transform lives and ruin lives. Time can bring people together or push people apart. Time is a resource that has untapped potential when fully realized.

So how do we take advantage of this time?

By being mindful. But how do we be mindful? We forget about the outside world and take time to develop ourselves and who we are deep down from our actual internal wants, desires, and dreams. We understand ourselves by centering ourselves and embracing the balance of yin and yang.

The problem is that some people are losing their sense of self because of societal pressures. According to a 2021 *Harvard Business Review* article, overworking oneself is not beneficial to the mind or body and can have adverse mental health effects. However, overcoming poor working habits and achieving a healthy work-life balance is very challenging. Most of the interviewees in HBR's survey admitted that their jobs are "demanding, exhausting, and chaotic." Is this because of the environment, or is this because of our mental state and perception? Most of the time, it is the latter. To overcome this self-imposed stress block, we must gain better self-awareness and redefine our role (Lupu and Ruiz-Castro 2021).

I wrote this book because I used to be an anxious perfectionist, crippled by ensuring every one of my moves was perfectly planned and executed. I used to be afraid to do many activities because I thought it was not worth the time or energy if it was not perfect. I also used to be mindless in my daily activities, not understanding that time leads me somewhere and that somewhere should be a destination I have thought about, not a destination that will welcome me unprepared.

When I became more religious and began to explore my faith while in college, especially during the COVID-19 pandemic, I simultaneously became more conscious of all my movements and desires. I understood that my life was a series of moments and choices. I understood I had the power to say no to people and choose what I wanted to do with my life. I understood that I have one life and should not want to waste any time doing activities that do not support my well-being or desires. The connection to my faith during the pandemic inspired my interest in meditation and yoga. I began to sit with my eyes closed in the sun, embracing the sun and just being present in nature. Meditation and yoga allowed me to remain grounded and humble, embracing equanimity like never before to understand that people and places will always come and go. Still, those external transformations should not change my center point.

Being in Asia for a year on the archipelago of Penghu in Taiwan allowed me to explore Asian culture, including

Confucian temples, Buddhist temples, Christian churches, and worship houses by beaches and inland. I got to understand what peace means to people in a different culture and explore the meanings behind the symbol that has implanted itself in world history forever: the yin-yang symbol.

The yin-yang symbol is an elusive and dynamic symbol representing the world of complementary forces coming together to create something bigger, better, and more robust. It means the connective tissue that binds us all as human beings with the air and stardust. It represents tai chi, which centers the body through expanding and contracting movements. It spreads us out to expose our soul and center our being in harmony.

Yin represents darkness, rest, the moon, and feminine energy while yang represents light, action, the sun, and masculine energy. Rather than compete with one another, the two colors blend with a bit of each within each other, allowing for wholeness and a cycle that is truly balanced and supportive of each side.

The duality of sides lives within people and pairs, creating masterpieces that take advantage of darkness and light, emptiness and fullness, inaction and action, and femininity and masculinity. Our world could not orbit around the sun without "the Dao" or "the way." The "chi" is the force that connects us all. It is omnipresent. According to the Tai Chi for Health Institute, tai chi means "supreme ultimate" because everything works together in unity beyond our sight (Lam 2022).

To reach our fullest potential, we must unlock a more proper and genuine form of ourselves by embracing mindfulness and the inner yin and yang inside, letting both the sponge and stone and the receptive and expressive sides of ourselves develop and take shape.

Becoming spiritual, no matter what religion, may help to ground oneself and find clarity in times of insecurity, stress, or difficulty. This commitment offers a lot because when we understand there is a greater power above anyone else and ourselves, we can put life into perspective and realize everything will work out how it should.

When we look closer at the highest quality of creation and being in life—from the TV and the cinema to the people around us—the duality within each creates intrigue, interest, and, ultimately, magic. Without rest, we would be unable to wake up and live this life together. Without the moon, there would be no sun. Without suffering, there would be no happiness. The duality represented by the dark and light sides of yin and yang explains that our vast world constantly changes rapidly.

How can we find harmony within our fast-paced world? Reflect on how you live and how you would want to change moving forward.

Some questions to consider are:

- Are you mindful?
- Do you take time out of your day to meditate?

- Can you decipher both the yin and yang aspects of yourself?
- Are you balanced?
- Are you spiritual?
- Do you feel you have a clear purpose in life, and does this purpose bring you joy and comfort daily?

We can only create a path forward for ourselves when we are truly honest with who we are—fully surrendering to the moment and our life's plan. The only changes we can make begin today. The only time we have to change the course of the future is now. There is no changing the past and no rushing toward a future, so enjoy today for what it is and what it offers. Love the people surrounding you and give all you have to live. Take patience, breathe one step at a time, and you will be alright.

Bonus Content

**JOURNAL FROM THE FIRST MONTH IN ASIA
(TAIPEI, MAGONG COUNTY, DANSHUI)**

*"To live intentionally, we must dig to the deepest why behind
the want."*

—*JAY SHETTY, THINK LIKE A MONK*

<u>First Day</u>

It is Wednesday, August 10, 2022, and I am quarantining in a
hotel called Green World Station in Taipei, Taiwan, on a Fulbright Scholarship to teach English in a Taiwanese classroom.
I arrived two days ago, on August 8, in the wee hours of the
morning, jet-lagged and exhausted. I am finally returning to
my normal state through coffee, some introductory courses,
and a Zumba class.

I decided to write my second book while in Asia because I
have much time to myself during this next year of teaching.
I will be busy most of the day and return home at night.

Religion and spirituality came to mind when thinking about what to write about. However, I wanted to explore an idea that went further and unpacked my surroundings while grasping life's meaning to me. I have always been intrigued by the duality of life: men and women, cats and dogs, day and night, SpongeBob and Patrick, Bonnie and Clyde, etcetera. This everlasting dynamic duo seems to reappear in any balanced state of existence. When thinking more about this, I thought about the ancient black-and-white symbol called yin yang created in China to measure the changing shadows in the solar year.

This mythical symbol has shown up throughout my life and has become a recurring motif for feelings of peace, Zen, and meditation. To me, yin and yang represent a state of balance and flow where nothing or no one can sway you or knock you down from your state of being. It denotes homeostasis within yourself and also in the world. When yin and yang are equally present, the world goes round smoothly, and people are happier and more efficient.

While sheltering on the Penghu islands off the southern coast of Taiwan for a year teaching English, I have decided to take a deeper look at the magnificent duality in our lives on Earth. In this search, I aspire to find answers to why harnessing this duality pushes boundaries and helps us create the best versions of ourselves.

<u>Second Day</u>

Today is Thursday, August 11, which marks my fourth morning in my suite at Green World Station. My four bottles of unopened yogurt in my fridge remind me of the days that pass. Now that I am fully back to my usual self with loads of rest, food, and time to recuperate and get used to my food and view, I have found Taiwan peaceful and beautiful. It is my sanctuary away from my busy California life of a continuously interrupted existence. While quarantining in my room, I found several empowering activities to take my time. I have started reading *Warrior* by Sam Liang. I have begun to study Mandarin more in depth. I had two classes yesterday on the subject: one on classroom conversations and the other on food in Taiwan. I also met English teaching assistants from previous years, who were incredibly warm and gave helpful advice. I take my temperature twice daily, once at 9 a.m. and once at 9 p.m.

I have begun brainstorming pieces for my next book about Earth's duality in nature. It has been exciting to look out my window and see the busy streets of Taiwan with motorized bikes and cars whizzing by quickly. It makes for nice noise when I wake up in the mornings, usually around 5 a.m. The coffee here is fantastic. I typically brew three packets in the morning, which comes out to about three cups. The coffee is creamy and very light. Already, I have begun to see balance represented around me. Colors in twos very prominently offset each other. Signs feature the colors green and yellow a lot. I also see the color combinations of orange, blue, black, and white. Every sign features two colors, and there are many signs.

Across from my hotel is another hotel called Relax 5, ironically similar to my Instagram handle, Razz5. When I sent a photo to my dad, he instantly said, "So relax!" He was referring to the Asian-owned massage shop we go to back home at the local mall where we live. I have sensed a better understanding of courtesy here and respecting each other's space and time. It is pretty nice. I think this respect allows people to be more independent. This balance is often different in the states, where many more people seem dependent on others and fall into the trap of stress and not fully being themselves.

I have already asked the front desk for more coffee bags because I love caffeine, and I cannot wait to start exploring the city and trying all the food. "Guàng yèshi" means walking in the night market. I learned that yesterday. I also learned that 7-Eleven is "Xiao Qi," which means "Little Seven." In the states, I would go to 7-Eleven all the time in the wee hours of the morning when I could not sleep to get my morning coffee. It is a great spot.

Yesterday, I also learned some funny Taiwanese sayings that are prominent. The first is "food is the god of the people." ~ "Mín yi shí wéi tián." The second is "Nothing is more important than eating." ~ "Chī fàn huáng dì da."

As a big food connoisseur, I was excited when I heard these sayings from Foreign Language Teaching Assistant Jessie Lee (Pei-Jen). I also found it hilarious that one way to introduce yourself to people can be, "Chī bao le ma?" Or "Are you full?" With an emphasis on food and respect within the culture, I already love my existence in Taiwan. It seems yin and yang are represented in many interesting ways. I cannot wait to explore those avenues when I make my way to the beautiful archipelago of Penghu (Pescadores Islands).

<u>Third Day</u>

Friday, August 12, marks the fifth day in my hotel room here at Green World Station. I can leave the hotel with my mask during the next four days of quarantine, including today. Today, at 4 a.m., I walked to Chiang Kai-Shek Memorial Hall to see the beautiful fields, long walkways, and extraordinary white and red buildings that memorialize Taiwan's long walk to freedom of speech. It was exhilarating and rewarding that on my first day in that city, I could see such a beautiful place that holds a lot of history and significance in the city of Taipei and the country of Taiwan as a whole.

While sitting and taking in my surroundings, I realized how unique this country is. It is exotic, known for its hot weather; progressive, pushing for the rights of all people; full of life, some of the best food in the world at their night markets; and filled with spirit. It took years to become independent from China. At 6 a.m., after my thirty-minute walk, I saw people doing their daily run, and I could see their persistence and hard work with every move in their bodies. I took in my surroundings for almost an hour before returning for my fifth Zoom training day.

I met Doctor Jared Pendleton, Maria Ting, and Counselor Evon Chiu yesterday. I also learned about the various acronyms involved in my job here in Taiwan. Today's sessions were about cultural diversity and the makeup of Taiwan's diversity. It was fascinating to get to know the country where I will be spending the next year of my life a little better. I think I will like her a lot.

<u>Fourth Day</u>

It is the weekend here: Saturday, August 13th! That means no training today. I have a full day to explore Taipei for the next two days before I leave on my flight to Penghu on Tuesday, August 16. I connected to some outstanding people of the Taiwan Church of Christ here, who generously picked me up this Sunday for morning church at 11 a.m.

Yesterday, I wrapped up my day with another gorgeous bento box. I watched *Friends with Benefits*, a few new stand-up comedians, and *Friends*—one of my all-time favorite shows—on Netflix. Relaxing in the afternoon after a long week in a new country with daily training was enjoyable. I went to sleep at around 6 p.m. and woke up at 2 a.m. I went out early this morning to check out 7-Eleven (Xiao Qi: Little Seven) in Taiwan for the first time. It differs from the 7-Eleven we have in the United States—other foods and designs. I bought taro chips since I am on a colossal taro wave right now and Original Green Peas. I am a big veggie guy. I noticed many 7-Elevens are also coupled with a Family Mart nearby. Interesting, given that they are seemingly competitors. This pairing is another example of duality in life. Often, similar stores and restaurants will couple up because they notice it may be a good spot for their type of business. Customers who do not have complete brand loyalty will check out both convenience stores when in the area when looking for particular snacks or goodies.

I am incredibly excited to check out a night market (yéshi) today. I also may check out Longshan Temple, a folk religious temple in Wanhua District, Taipei, combination of Taoism and Buddhism with a Confucian worldview. I also want to check out a park in the Wanhua District called Longshan Riverside Park, which has a beautiful view of the Tamsui River and Zhongxing Bridge.

<u>Fifth Day</u>

Yesterday was a beautiful day of exploration. It was ninety degrees until sundown. That is the obscure thing about Taiwan. It is always hot. It feels like living in a simulation. I just returned from church with the people who created the Taiwan Church of Christ (TCOC). I met several disciples in the ministry there, and they treated me to a beautiful authentic Chinese roundtable lunch. I had grilled spicy chicken, fried tofu, seaweed, vegetables and egg wraps, and sweet bread.

The church was incredibly welcoming, and the service was almost two hours long. They were gracious enough to have translators for me, which was beautiful. The sermon was outstanding, and the communion talk was hilarious about being a bridesmaid. The lady giving the speech reminded me of how meaningful a wedding is when it is held in a church and based on religion with God's grace and eye. This service and the outstanding hospitality by so many Taipei locals blew my mind. They once again reminded me of the warmth of the people within the city. The balance of humility and drive in the Taiwanese people is unbelievable. I was so impressed with all their questions and interest in my life as if I were their son. They continued calling me their son and demanding that they would be there for me if I needed anything. They truly made me feel at home.

I think yin and yang in social circles are when there is a consistent balance between everyone while everyone also feels challenged. I appreciated that dynamic with my disciple friends in the church, who all naturally felt like my second parents.

The weather here is also a representation of balance. While it is humid and sticky, it is also cloudy and windy. Yesterday, the sun was beaming down while visiting the majestic Longshan Temple. I appreciated the practice of folk religion, which is also a delicate balance of Buddhism, Taoism, and Confucianism—a blend that significantly connects the yin-yang symbol. The balance of opposites was displayed in the sky and worship. I returned to my hotel after walking along the river at Longshan Riverside Park.

<u>Sixth Day</u>

Today, Monday, August 15, I got up at 12 a.m. I slept at about 7 p.m., my usual time here in Taipei. When I woke up, I walked over to 7-Eleven to purchase a bag of PopCorners Sweet & Salty chips and a latte (Ná tiě). I began watching *Big Time Adolescence*, starring Pete Davidson, Griffin Gluck, and Machine Gun Kelly. I also published two more episodes of my Kindle Vella Series—one of Restaurateur Philip Camino and one on the ideation behind In Food We Trust: Food and Justice, the podcast and video cast Tara Elaine Brennan and I were thinking about. All the Penghu Fulbrighters then introduced themselves, and I found out that my school would be Peng Nan Junior High.

I walked the city after a delicious chicken, egg, and rice bowl. I ordered an almond ice cream bar before returning to Green World Station as the rain started to beat down hard. I began packing and preparing for my flight to my permanent base tomorrow in the Penghu Islands.

To Penghu, I fly…

<u>Seventh and Eighth Days</u>

Yesterday, Tuesday, August 16, was an odd day. I woke up early again and ordered one latte (yībei ná tie) at the 7-Eleven. I then finished watching this brilliant film with Jack Nicholson and Diane Keaton called *Something's Gotta Give*. I started some teaching with electronics training. Then I visited Heritage Cafe and tried their avocado tacos and a banana passion tart. It was delicious. I took a taxi to Songshan Airport, a regional airport and military airbase. I flew to Penghu on a puddle jumper with seat A1. I landed in the Penghu Islands—eighty-degree tropical paradise. I taxied to my new permanent home on Beichen Street in Magong City with my coordinator, Anny Chen. I met my roommate, Gabo, who took a headshot for Fulbright's professional keeping and did a grocery run. I then got dinner with fellow second-year Fulbright Malka at a local restaurant, where I ordered peanut sauce noodles. We discussed religion, creative expression, and home in the states. She then drove me back home on her motorcycle. I passed out immediately and woke up the next day to walk to watch the sunrise.

At 5 a.m., I walked to Magong First Fishing Harbor to catch the 5:38 a.m. sunrise. It was beautiful, filled with striking colors of pink, orange, purple, and blue. It was a beautiful moment and an incredible way to spend my first morning in my new home for the following year. I walked back home and into my air-conditioned room. I then made some banana and peanut butter toast and watched some morning talk shows before renewing my California Insurance License. Today, I will work on the hardcover edition of my book *Fine Dining*, set up my Trojan Network Profile, and prepare to go to my school tomorrow, Peng Nan Junior High.

<u>Ninth Day</u>

I am fully settled on the Penghu Islands in Magong City on Beichen Street today. My roommate is Gabo, an Argentinian who went to the University of Washington Saint Louis in Missouri; he is a great guy. We worked out last night at the local gym called Joker. Before working out, we got dinner at a local restaurant where we ordered chicken soup, duck soup, fried sweet potato, and churros. It was an incredibly delicious meal. I cannot wait to try more seafood on the island and visit more restaurants.

I woke up at my usual 5 a.m. this morning and walked to Magong Harbor to watch the beautiful sunrise. I will begin more research on the yin-yang symbol through in-depth research on the temples here. Yesterday, I applied for my Alien Resident Certificate with my site coordinator, Anny. She also showed me around town, specifically the state-of-the-art Penghu Stadium with a beautiful track and gym. I also saw the many gorgeous temples around town, shining with bright red, orange, and gold colors.

Today, I am doing my first in-person training at Wenguang Elementary School. Gabo and I will walk there. Before that, I will enjoy my banana and peanut butter on toast and watch some news shows to see what is happening back home. Then, I will do more research on yin and yang. I also am starting an old movie from 2011 called *What's Your Number?* starring Chris Evans and Anna Faris.

Tenth Day

Today is Friday! Yesterday was a very productive day for me. After training, I met my LET, a thirty-two-year-old Taiwanese local named Merry, and my school's principal, Bruce. My school seems very fun with foosball, wind-surfing boards, science rooms, and a big auditorium called the audio-visual room. After that, I returned to my Magong City apartment and ultimately passed out. I woke up for an interview with Restaurant Rockstars at 8 p.m. and then went back to sleep immediately.

I woke up at my usual 5 a.m. and slowly got up for the day. I showered and got dressed for a beautiful day in the city. I walked down to the harbor to watch the sunrise while getting a latte at 7-Eleven on the way. I watched *LIVE with Kelly and Ryan* on YouTube, featuring Jake Gyllenhaal, and then checked out the beautiful local temple and Four Points hotel. After my mini exploration, I returned to my place to meet with Gabo to walk to training. Today was Gabo's twenty-third birthday. During training on listening and speaking and classroom dynamics with the LET, our coordinators presented Gabo with some bakery items from a local bakery. After returning from training at Wenguang Elementary, we returned to Joker to work out. Then we headed to a local restaurant to meet with the other Penghu Fulbrighters for a nice birthday dinner.

<u>Eleventh Day</u>

Today is Saturday, August 20, English Day (Camp Day) at Peng Nan Junior High, my school for the year. I woke up around 2 a.m. today to some messages from my publisher regarding my new book and working out my *Fine Dining* hardcover book cover design and pricing. I quickly finished that work and then messaged Tanya Holland and Maya Blackstone about their feedback and thoughts on my work. I decided I did not feel like going back to sleep, so I made some famous banana and peanut butter on the bread before going downtown and to the harbor this morning. Luckily, Rae, my local coordinator, will pick me up at the Far EasTone store at 7:35 a.m. to get to the school by 8 a.m.

The training day went so well! I was paired with Lexi and met my Peng Nan coteacher, Leo. We did three sessions of Janken with eight different English phrases with each group. It was so fun and refreshing. Afterward, my school's principal Bruce and a teacher treated us to a beautiful lunch at QingWan360. I ordered Shrimp Pasta with XO Sauce with pumpkin soup and iced oolong tea here. We also received cactus ice cream after our meal. Then Bruce showed us the island on the gorgeous balcony, pointing out the other two big islands in Penghu. The restaurant was at Penghu International Diving Center, so there were infinity pools and a seven-meter pool to practice diving. When I returned, I had some local pastries from a bakery that they gifted us on

English Day (Camp Day), took a long nap, and made some peanut butter and banana on bread.

<u>Sunday and Monday (August 21 and August 22)</u>

Sunday was such a fun day. I went to the Pier 3 Mall, checked out a restaurant called Teishoku 8, and ordered a beautiful fishbowl with rice. I saw a matinee at the theatre: *Bullet Train* starring Brad Pitt with several other cameos. I enjoyed the movie and ordered honey cashews and Sweet & Salty Pop-Corners chips. I took a long walk around the harbor and then came home to sleep early.

On Monday, I woke up early to publish a couple of Kindle Vella episodes, and then I decided to work out at Joker and walk to the beach. It was eighty-five degrees outside, so I came back to enjoy my day off by watching movies. I finished *Good on Paper* and started *Senior Year*, a new Netflix original starring Rebel Wilson. I plan to go to Freud Pub tonight to order their famous six-drink cocktail called "Absolute Drunk" to celebrate the start of my birthday at midnight!

<u>August 23: My Twenty-Second Birthday in Penghu</u>

Today was my twenty-second birthday. I woke up around 5 a.m. hungover from drinking an "Absolute Drunk," six alcoholic drinks from Freud Pub, last night and a Taiwanese beer. I woke up and went to 7-Eleven to purchase a peanut butter sandwich. I cut up some bananas to put on top of the sandwich. I then went to the market to get an apple. I returned and finished watching *Look Both Ways*, a Netflix movie starring Lili Reinhart. As I was coming back, a friend from home called me named Matthew Bui and we FaceTimed for about thirty minutes as he got ready for his next dental school class—my first birthday call.

I then walked over to a breakfast spot called My Shine Station, where I ordered a quiche, egg, and onion pancake. I returned home and got a call from my parents and brother wishing me a happy birthday. I showered and then my on-site coordinator, named Anny, called me to tell me she was ready to take my roommate and me to the Taiwan Bank to set up our bank accounts with our new alien resident cards.

After that, Gabo and I went to Sushi Express, located in Pier 3, where we chowed down on some quality sushi from a conveyor belt. The oysters, filled with delectable rice and cheese, were a highlight. When we got back, we both napped for a while. When I got up, I returned to Pier 3 to purchase Puma athletic clothes. I then walked over to a well-known ice cream place on the island called 23.5 Degrees Cactus Ice Cream, where I ordered shaved milk ice with cactus sorbet, boba balls, and tea ice cream. I walked over to the other side of the island by the bridge to watch the sun go down, and then I headed back to my place to shower. I will hit a bar tonight to have a drink and ring in my birthday in America. We will check out Suave Bar, located in the Sheraton Four Points Hotel lobby by Magong Harbor. Instead, I ordered some Taro balls from Fat Daddy Fried Chicken. I then watched *Identity Thief* and called it a night for an early flight back to Taipei for on-site orientation. The celebration never ends!

<u>Wednesday–Friday (August 24–August 26)</u>

I woke up at midnight to experience my birthday in America! Then we took a cab to the airport at 7:30 a.m. from our apartment to fly back to Taipei. When we landed, we took bus 6 to New Taipei City to stay at Fullon Tamsui Fisherman's Wharf, a five-star hotel by the water. It was gorgeous. We spent the first day at a welcome day and training.

I went to sleep very early and then woke up at about 4 a.m. on Thursday to enjoy the gorgeous sunrise on the Danshui River and see the beautiful lights of The Lover's Bridge. Thursday was a long training day, from 9:30 a.m. with breakfast starting at 7 a.m. to 8:30 p.m. We began with an opening, an AIT Welcome, Identity in a New Cultural Context by Doctor Kelli Swazey and dissecting *Beyond Beauty*—a documentary by gifted filmmaker Mr. Chi Po-Lin. We had a lovely chicken bento box lunch and then did two survival teaching kits with our peers. After another break, we watched a DEI panel. We finished with a delicious family-style dinner and a fun cultural night with a fruit game.

On Friday, I woke up at 2:30 a.m. after going to sleep at 9 p.m. I walked around the hotel and got a large iced latte from 7-Eleven and a Coke Zero Sugar Fiber+. We returned our room keys at 9:15 a.m. after some breakfast where I had espresso with milk tea and porridge with peanuts and raisins. The bus drove us thirty minutes to Fort San Domingo. We stayed there for about an hour and learned about the British Council's lifetime at the base. We then drove to the American Club for about an hour, where we enjoyed an incredible lunch.

After lunch, I visited Shirley at Radio Taiwan International. She gave Gabo and me a long tour. We received a bus ride back to Taipei Songshan Airport. Gabo and I Ubered to our home for the next two days (Hotel Éclat, Taipei) before returning to Penghu for the first day of school. Tonight, we are checking out a local restaurant and famous food market, Shilin Night Market. My church/actor friend Charles is meeting and showing us around the city. We passed out and had to rain-check our meetup with Charles.

<u>Saturday, August 27–Monday, August 29</u>

Today was extraordinary in Daan District. I walked to Taipei 101 to check out the talk of the town. Before getting there, I stopped for a foot massage and shoulder rub. It was much needed. The owner asked if I could give her English lessons. I told her I was soon off to Penghu, so that might be difficult. She insisted on Zoom. I may take her up on it. When I got to Taipei 101, I saw all the great stores—from Ralph Lauren and Yves Saint Laurent to Gucci. The tallest building in Taipei was clean and gorgeous. I walked back to get ready for a night at Marco Polo Lounge in Shangri-La Hotel, MUME, and dessert from Eastern Ice Store courtesy of our new friends Wei and Wei, who also took us to Shuang Hsiang Yuan Tea House.

They brought us directly back to our hotel. The next day, Sunday, we flew back to Penghu. I ordered breakfast at a beautiful place called Brun before taking the Uber to the airport with Gabo. When we returned, we visited the grocery store. I then went for a night walk to the island's northern part and returned to have a few bananas and peanut butter toast before sleeping at 8 p.m.. The next day, Monday, I planned to publish a Kindle Vella article on Doctor Varun Soni, my spiritual mentor, and study for my written driver's test to achieve the first step on the quest for my scooter license. Luckily, for the first week of school, Bruce, Peng Nan Junior High's principal, drives me from downtown Magong every morning at 6:50 a.m. to get to school. I am grateful. My LET, Merry, sent me my weekly schedule, which features seventeen lessons starting at 7:30 a.m. on Mondays. To celebrate the last night before my big first day, I ordered squid pizza from Mercato Pizza, which is slowly becoming my favorite restaurant on the island.

<u>August 30, First Day of School</u>

I woke up at 3:30 a.m. to attend a script analysis class by Sandra K. Horner at 4 a.m. I then attended a Houde School of Acting class audit by Jessica Morris.

Bruce, Peng Nan Junior High Principal, picked me up from 7-Eleven next to my apartment at 6:50 a.m. to go to school early. We chatted, he gave me a tour of the school, and then he gave me a gift of tea, coffee, a coffee maker, and fancy utensils. I prepared for my two classes for the day: eighth-grade English and ninth-grade English. Then after those two classes with lunch in between, Bruce took me to a biking shop to buy a bike so I could ride it to and from school. Biking, one of my favorite activities in the world, is something I have missed considerably while on this island. I plan to work out much tonight and prepare for a great day of teaching tomorrow: PE and reading club.

My first lunch at my school featured vegetable soup, white rice, grilled tofu, and chicken legs. It was delicious, as I did not eat breakfast that morning. I ate two chicken legs and quite a bit of tofu with rice. I also ate a banana and was ready for the rest of the day. I rested when I returned to my apartment before working out, making fried eggs on toast, and passing out.

<u>August 31, Second Day of School</u>

Today, I woke up at 3 a.m., made some coffee, and ran to 7-Eleven to purchase a Coke Zero Sugar Fiber+ and some bananas. I had a couple of eggs on toast and toast with peanut butter and banana. Bruce picked me up at 6:50 again from the 7-Eleven. When we got to school, I chatted with Bruce about his career, the symbol of security and love that tiles represent, Fong Ru Tea, and the fact that there are fifty other schools in Penghu. He knows most of the principals and more.

I am learning a lot about the culture here through my relationship with Bruce and Merry, two very considerate and profound individuals. Today, I have PE class and a reading class after lunch. It is a more lowkey day today, allowing me to relax and settle into daily life at Peng Nan Junior High while journaling and reading my Bible. I had a lot of white rice with tofu, spinach, and vegetable soup for lunch. Right around 4 p.m., I get tired and cannot wait to nap and relax. Leo, one of my English co-teachers for eighth and ninth grade, drove me back home after school. I walked to Magong First Fishing Harbor and saw Argo Sail Yacht Club on Shooting the Breeze Cafe. Then I walked back home and passed out.

<u>September 1</u>

Today is my third day teaching at school. Thursdays are by far my busiest days at school. I have international education, three English classes in a row—ninth, seventh, eighth—and then PE and another English class after lunch. This day will test my endurance. Most kids are exhausted by midday, so we will see how I feel throughout the day. What is remarkable is that my reward is a Friday with only PE after my early international education class. I have decided to introduce a new food and region from the world each week as part of the international education teaching. I will explore different books for the reading club, starting with *Weird but True Foods*. At school today, I had a big lunch of chicken, hard-boiled eggs, white rice, and chicken soup. It was delicious. After finishing up PE and my last class of the day—ninth-grade English over Zoom—I got back home via scooter with one of the teachers at the school. He showed me the place where I would take my scooter test. When I returned, I made a peanut butter and banana on bread snack, took a nap, made some egg on bread, then started watching a movie called *Love in the Villa*. I went to sleep around 9 p.m.

Other movies I watched during the rest of my year in Penghu: *Don't Worry Darling*, *Bones and All*, *Amsterdam*, *Babylon*, *Misanthrope* or *To Catch a Killer*, *Guardians of the Galaxy Vol. 3*, *Fast and Furious X*, *Spider-Man: Across the Spider-Verse*, and *Stutz*.

Shows I enjoyed in Penghu: *Black Mirror* (Season 6) and *Headspace Guide to Meditation*.

My favorite Taiwanese foods: sushi, oyster omelets, scallion pancakes, sweet potato balls, seafood congee, oden (fish cake), radish cake, sesame balls, sago with coconut milk, Taiwanese shaved ice (bào bīng), and taro mochi.

My favorite Taiwanese drinks: taro milk tea with pearls from Milksha, Fong Ru Tea, watermelon juice, and Gold Medal Taiwan Beer.

2023 International Fireworks Festival

BBQ with Taiwanese Locals

BBQ with new Taiwan friends

Caesar Metro Hotel in Taipei

Car passenger with Milksha Drink (Taro Milk with Pearls)

Chimei Museum in Tainan

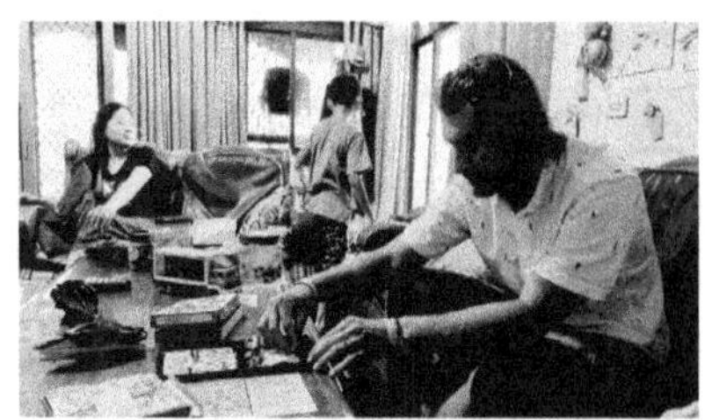

Chinese checkers in Xiyu

Chinese class

Dragon Boat Festival

Classroom with Moonlight water bottle and new book

Cloudenjoy B&B in Hualien County

Enjoying sunrise on my 22nd birthday

National Penghu University (where I took Chinese class)

Oregin Tea

Parents visiting Peng Nan Junior High

Sheraton Four Points BBQ

Sheraton Four Points Lobby

Sheraton Four Points Penghu Mascot

Sheraton Four Points BBQ,
enjoying Corona Beer

Summer Pizza Party

Shili Beach
(one of my favorite spots in the archipelago)

Wang An Cafe

The oceanside path I often walked along

Windsurfing

Acknowledgments

While writing this book, I was inspired by many people: Thich Nhat Hanh, *The Miracle of Mindfulness*; Antony Cummins, *The Ultimate Guide to Yin Yang*; Sadhguru, *Inner Engineering: A Yogi's Guide to Joy, A Taste of Well-Being: Sadhguru's Insights for Your Gastronomics*; Robin R. Wang, *Yinyang: The Way of Heaven and Earth in Chinese Thought and Culture*. These scholars inspired me to explore the intersections of mindfulness and personal peace/happiness, spirituality and balance, and duality and unity.

Transformational Coach Michael McDonald pointed out two fantastic books that inspire his work and mine: *Holy Noticing: The Bible, Your Brain, and the Mindful Space Between Moments* by Charles Stone and *Mindfulness* by Ellen Langer.

In Sadhguru's powerful July 14, 2020 discussion of "How to Manifest What You Really Want," he delineates pleasantness in four forms: body, health and pleasure; mind, peace and joy; emotion, love and compassion; and energy, blissfulness and ecstasy (Sadhguru 2020).

Suppose all these four forms work in one unified direction in our life toward personal peace. In that case, our ability to create is endless. Sadhguru's wisdom contributed significantly to diving into my mindfulness and peering more profoundly into the world around me.

I want to thank Peng Nan Junior High Bilingual Academy for welcoming me into their school with open arms and genuine care. Not only could I dictate how and what I wanted to teach, but all the teachers were amiable, wanting to show me around the city and share details about Taiwan. I will miss Principal Bruce, Ms. Merry, Mr. Tsai, Mr. Tommy, Mr. Leo, Mr. Xǔ Yán Chéng, Ms. Wú Qiū Xiāng, Ms. Zhào Zhǐ Hán, and Coach Liào Zhé Yì very much.

I also want to thank my talented editors, Regina Stribling and Anne Kelley, for their attention to detail and curiosity about my story. Thank you to Jordan Waterwash, Kristy Carter, Kelley Wilson, Eric Koester, Gjorgji Pejkovski, Milan Krstevski, and Amanda Brown for helping me along my publishing journey.

Thanks to my family and close friends in California: Dad, Mom, Luke, Bill, Suz, Erik, Erin, Kristen, Wes, Cash, Capri, Jon, Q, Evan, Parth, and Bui. I appreciate you.

Many thanks to the supportive people in my circle during my writing process: Kenai Class for the massage recommendations and being my Dragon Boat partner, Reese Bergschneider for the homemade pumpkin pie and Kathy's Kitchen Pineapple Salsa, Kelly Han for her Chocolate Peanut Butter Oatmeal Bars (key to my heart), Owen Zoll for being a great

DJ, Maiya Peterson for challenging me in Chinese, Olivia Bates for hosting a Dirty Santa party, Maggie Wu for producing a documentary, Rubani Walia for organizing a Thanksgiving Potluck, Teresa Kuo for creating an end-of-year poster, Alexia Sales for offering me many movie recommendations, Brenda Coromina for managing after-school basketball, Gerardy Jean-Philippe II for the many Taiwanese facts, Lexi Kerstetter for introducing me to Penghu's beautiful Subway, Theresa Darroch for the candle recommendations, Malka Schnaidman for always making me smile, Gabriel Chaffee for being a great roommate, Anny Chen for helping me survive in a foreign country, Rae Fu for her state-of-the-art pizza oven and her calming presence, Deborah Broomer and Dejah Crystal for being extraordinary advisors, and Yu Fang Lin and Amie Yun Hsin Kuo for offering advanced perspectives on mental health.

A few enlightening books I read for fuel while living in Penghu include *The Magic of Surrender* by Kute Blackman, *Atlas of the Heart* by Brené Brown, *Conscience* by Patricia S. Churchland, *Above the Line* by Stephen Klemich and Mara Klemich, *Clarity & Connection* by Yung Pueblo, *Do Nothing* by Celeste Headlee, *Chatter* by Ethan Kross, *Religion and the Meaning of Life* by Clifford Williams, *Welcome Home* by Najwa Zebian, *Supernormal* by Meg Jay, PhD, *Being You* by Anil Seth, and *The Creative Act* by Rick Rubin. I also want to acknowledge the magical coffee shops on the archipelago that I frequented: Nikoni, 880 Café, Montecarlo Cafe, Louisa Coffee, Donutes, Shili Cafe, Wang An Cafe, and Gilly Primavera Cafe.

Finally, I want to acknowledge and express my gratitude to the readers who chose to preorder my book during the pre-sale process. Thank you for being the first to show interest in my story. This group includes:

Adlai Wertman
Annamarie Fernyak
Ariel Miller
Catherine Kavanaugh
Cathy Norman
Dana Pipkin
David Peters
Denise Hantsch
Dr. Ginny A Baro
Eric Koester
Gregg Rasmussen
Heather Howard Bloom
Helen (Missy) Kurpiewski
Ingrid Strotman
Jacob Ardron
Jeanette Rasmussen
Jon Rasmussen
Kari Brown
Kathy Goodin
Leanne Seavers
Lenette Chun
Linda Crandall
Lisa Starr
Lorena Pedraza
Luke Rasmussen
Maliik Morales
Matthew Bui

Michael Crisafulli

Nicholas D'Souza

Nina Lamour

Paul Tashiro

Stacey Dougherty

Stephanie Seng

Summer Short

Susie Fazlollahi

Teri and John Grosey

Thomas Chaffee

Zach Norcia

As well as others who chose to remain anonymous.

Appendix

CHAPTER 1: INTRODUCTION TO TAIWAN

Kabat-Zinn, Jon. 2011. "Jon Kabat-Zinn—'The Healing Power of Mindfulness.'" Dartmouth. April 13, 2011. 1:52:32. https://www.youtube.com/watch?v=_If4a-gHg_I.

Maté, Gabor. 2019. "Dr. Gabor Maté on the Connection between Stress and Disease." How To Academy Mindset. August 15, 2019. 1:16:45. https://www.youtube.com/watch?v=ajo3xkhTbfo.

Sadhguru. 2021. "Matthew McConaughey in Conversation with Sadhguru {Full Talk}." Sadhguru. June 2, 2021. 1:03:13. https://www.youtube.com/watch?v=IAoffyn2xpM.

UnivDatos Market Insights. 2021. "Mindfulness Meditation Apps Market Report, Share & Size, Analysis 2021-2027." Market Research Reporting & Analysis Agency in India. Accessed October 1, 2022. https://univdatos.com/report/mindfulness-meditation-apps-market/.

Vago, David. 2017. "Self-Transformation through Mindfulness | Dr. David Vago | Tedxnashville." TEDx Talks. April 24, 2017. 19:34. https://www.youtube.com/watch?v=1nP5oedmzkM.

CHAPTER 2: INTRODUCTION TO YIN AND YANG: DARKNESS AND DAYLIGHT

Einzelgänger. 2019. "The Deep Meaning of Yin & Yang." Einzelgänger. September 7, 2019. 11:12. https://www.youtube.com/watch?v=6gIMVxFen_A.

Laozi and Man-Ho Kwok. 1995. *Tao Te Ching*. Berlin: Theseus Verl.

Mead, Cat. 2021. "The Duality of Yin & Yang." *Yin: Untangled—Yin Yoga with Cat Mead*. February 16, 2021. 15:18. https://open.spotify.com/episode/33GoSdJWsWHk12v6NGm5Lg?si=2v7Z7eEX-QQee1EwwegmJYA.

Tzu Chi Foundation. 2014. "About Tzu Chi." Tzu Chi Foundation. June 6, 2014. https://www.tzuchi-org.tw/en/index.php?option=com_content&view=section&layout=blog&id=5&Itemid=181&lang=en.

Wilde, Olivia, director. 2022. *Don't Worry Darling*. Warner Bros. Pictures. 2 hr., 3 min. https://www.hbo.com/movies/dont-worry-darling.

Wilde, Olivia. 2022. "'Don't Worry Darling' Press Conference—79th Venice International Film Festival." Titanium Magazine. September 5, 2022. 12:16. https://www.youtube.com/watch?v=qZZmpNLa_eY.

CHAPTER 3: BONES: TAI CHI AND MYTHOLOGY

Brindley, Erica. 2023. *Individualism in Classical Chinese Thought*. Internet Encyclopedia of Philosophy. https://iep.utm.edu/ind-chin/.

Cartwright, Mark. 2018. *Yin and Yang*. World History Encyclopedia. United Kingdom: World History Publishing. https://www.worldhistory.org/Yin_and_Yang/.

Jahnke, Roger. 2016. "The Physiology of Tai Chi and QiGong." The Tai Chi and Qigong Way. August 11, 2016. 12:04. https://www.youtube.com/watch?v=ZJRtZAwVwgo.

Lam, Paul. 2022. "What Is Tai Chi & What Are the Health Benefits? (Complete Guide)." Tai Chi for Health Institute. Accessed October 15, 2022. https://taichiforhealthinstitute.org/what-is-tai-chi/.

CHAPTER 4: RICH SPIRIT: TAOISM (DAOISM), BUDDHISM, CONFUCIANISM, AND CHRISTIANITY

Amadeus. 2020. "Taoism Explained" Cognito. August 29, 2020. 20:04. https://www.youtube.com/watch?v=U6hslRjGaww.

BBC Teach. 2021. "Why Do Buddhists Meditate?" *GCSE Religious Studies* (blog), BBC. August 19, 2021. https://www.bbc.co.uk/teach/why-do-buddhists-meditate/zdt9f4j#:~:text=Meditation%20is%20one%20of%20the,%3B%20loving%2Dkindness%20and%20visualisation.

Bellaimey, John. 2013. "The Hidden Meanings of Yin and Yang—John Bellaimey." *TEDEd Animation* (blog), TEDEd. August 2,

2013. https://ed.ted.com/lessons/the-hidden-meanings-of-yin-and-yang-john-bellaimey.

Berling, Judith A. 2023. "Confucianism." Asia Society. Accessed November 1, 2022. https://asiasociety.org/education/confucianism.

Laozi and Man-Ho Kwok. 1995. *Tao Te Ching.* Berlin, Germany: Theseus Verl.

The Editors of Encyclopaedia Britannica. 2009. *San-ch'ing.* Britannica Global Edition. Chicago, Illinois: Encyclopædia Britannica. https://www.britannica.com/topic/San-ching.

Wu, Sofia. 2009. "Feature: Temple Painting Becomes a Fading Art." *Taipei Times,* 台北時報. February 12, 2009. https://www.taipeitimes.com/News/taiwan/archives/2009/02/13/2003435971.

Yong, Ced. 2023. "108 Chinese Mythological Gods and Characters (2023 Edition)." *Owlcation,* April 12, 2023. https://owlcation.com/humanities/chinese-mythological-gods-characters.

CHAPTER 5: MIRRORS…
Cartwright, Mark. 2018. *Yin and Yang.* World History Encyclopedia. United Kingdom: World History Publishing. https://www.worldhistory.org/Yin_and_Yang/.

Hill, Jonah, director. 2022. *Stutz.* Netflix. 1 hr., 36 min. https://www.netflix.com/title/81387962.

Shan, Jun. 2020. "The Meaning of Yin and Yang." *ThoughtCo.* February 3, 2020. https://www.thoughtco.com/ yin-and-yang-629214#:~:text=Yin%20and%20yang%20(or%20 yin,can%20be%20observed%20in%20nature.

Swaim, Emily. 2022. "7 Reminders to Carry with You on Your Trauma Recovery Journey." *Healthline.* May 25, 2022. https:// www.healthline.com/health/mental-health/trauma-recovery- #recovery-has-stages.

CHAPTER 6: THE CRIPPLING WORKAHOLIC TRADITION: NEVER SLEEP

Baumann, C., and H. Winzar. 2017. "Chapter 3—Confucianism and Work Ethic—Introducing the ReVaMB Model." In *The Political Economy of Business Ethics in East Asia: A Historical and Comparative Perspective*, edited by Ingyu Oh and Kil-sŏng Pak, 33–70. Amsterdam, Netherlands: Chandos Publishing.

Center for Creative Leadership. 2022. "How to Instill a Coaching Culture." CCL. Accessed November 15, 2022. https://www.ccl. org/articles/leading-effectively-articles/instill-coaching-cul- ture/.

Durvasula, Ramani. 2023. "Confronting Complex PTSD with Stephanie Foo." *Navigating Narcissism with Dr. Ramani.* April 13, 2023. 1:08:03. https://open.spotify.com/episode/0YW6Ny- 8Mue8nBH5emipAyE?si=ENjnv4iOTdih34fga_bLog.

Forbes Coaches Council. 2022. "15 Effective Strategies for Main- taining Company Culture during Key Leadership Changes." *Forbes,* December 26, 2022. https://www.forbes.com/ sites/forbescoachescouncil/2022/12/26/15-effective-strategies-for-maintaining-company-culture-during-key-leadership-changes/?sh=66d10019354b.

Hashimoto, Akiko, and Charlotte Ikels. 2005. "Chapter 5.5—Filial Piety in Changing Asian Societies." In *The Cambridge Handbook of Age and Ageing,* edited by Malcolm L. Johnson, 437–442. Cambridge: Cambridge University Press. https://www.cambridge.org/core/books/abs/cambridge-handbook-of-age-and-ageing/filial-piety-in-changing-asian-societies/A47E009121CBEC57517BFADF7AAF3C66.

Psychology Today Staff. 2023. "Burnout." *Psychology Today.* Accessed November 15, 2022. https://www.psychologytoday.com/us/basics/burnout.

CHAPTER 7: SPIRITUAL TRANSCENDENCE: ISLAS PESCADORES

roundTAIWANround. 2015. "Yin Yang Sea in Jiufen." roundTAIWANround. Accessed November 15, 2022. https://www.rtaiwanr.com/jiufen/ying-yang-sea.

Sadhguru. 2021. "Crafting Destiny, Exploring the Unknown." The Library of Consciousness. June 2, 2021. www.organism.earth/library/document/crafting-destiny-exploring-unknown.

Sadhguru. 2021. "Matthew McConaughey in Conversation with Sadhguru {Full Talk}." Sadhguru. June 2, 2021. 1:03:13. https://www.youtube.com/watch?v=IAoffyn2xpM.

Sun Moon Lake National Scenic Area Administration. 2019. "Discover Sun Moon Lake." Sun Moon Lake National Scenic Area.

Accessed November 15, 2022. https://www.sunmoonlake.gov.
tw/en.

**CHAPTER 8: LIVE LIFE LIKE A SPONGE RATHER THAN A SPRIN-
KLER, BUT ALSO LIKE A STONE**

Blackson, Kute. 2022. *The Magic of Surrender: Finding the Courage
to Let Go.* New York: ATarcherPerigee Book, an Imprint of
Penguin Random House LLC.

Brooten-Brooks, Michelle C. 2022. "The Psychology behind Excessive Talking." *Verywell Health*, April 27, 2022. https://www.
verywellhealth.com/excessive-talking-5224128.

Drymon, Derek and Stephen Hillenburg, directors. 1999. *Sponge-
Bob SquarePants.* Season 1, Episode 1, "Help Wanted." Written
by Stephen Hillenburg, Derek Drymon, and Tim Hill. Aired
on May 1, 1999 on Nickelodeon. https://www.amazon.com/
SpongeBob-SquarePants-Season-1/dp/B00oHJ4WLC.

Forbes Leadership Forum. 2012. "To Be a Great Leader, Don't Be a
Genius; Be a Sponge and a Stone." *Forbes*, July 5, 2012. https://
www.forbes.com/sites/forbesleadershipforum/2011/09/15/
to-be-a-great-leader-dont-be-a-genius-be-a-sponge-and-a-
stone/?sh=4a2c9c4b586b.

Zenger, Jack, and Joseph Folkman. 2016. "What Great Listeners
Actually Do." *Harvard Business Review*, July 14, 2016. https://
hbr.org/2016/07/what-great-listeners-actually-do.

CHAPTER 9: THROUGH SUFFERING, LIFE MATTERS EXPONENTIALLY

Jay, Meg. 2017. *Supernormal: The Untold Story of Adversity and Resilience.* New York, NY: Twelve.

ONE Research Foundation—Official. 2020. "Stressed—A Documentary Film | 4K Official." ONE Research Foundation—Official. April 18, 2020. 1:02:28. https://www.youtube.com/watch?v=ahU2FP_b9OQ.

Pate, Joshua. 2019. "The Mysterious Science of Pain—Joshua w. Pate." TEDEd. May 20, 2019. https://www.youtube.com/watch?v=eakyDiXX6Uc.

Rapaport, Mark Hyman. 2012. "The Biological Benefits of Frequent Massage." Emory University. September 17, 2012. 3:20. https://www.youtube.com/watch?v=49Hq_-_KcJo.

Rinpoche, Mingyur. 2014. "Getting to Know Suffering." Yongey Mingyur Rinpoche. February 6, 2014. 5:57. https://www.youtube.com/watch?v=XSU6AooM4yk.

CHAPTER 10: NATURE, NURTURE, NADA

Cherry, Kendra. 2022. "The Nature vs. Nurture Debate." *Verywell Mind,* October 19, 2022. https://www.verywellmind.com/what-is-nature-versus-nurture-2795392#:~:text=Nurture-,The%20nature%20vs.,naturally%20regardless%20of%20environmental%20influences.

Dweck, Carol. 2016. *Mindset: The New Psychology of Success.* New York: Random House.

Huang, Al Chung-liang. 2011. *Embrace Tiger, Return to Mountain: The Essence of Tai Ji*. London: Singing Dragon.

Kwik, Jim, and Mark Hyman. 2020. *Limitless: Upgrade Your Brain, Learn Anything Faster, and Unlock Your Exceptional Life*. Alexandria, New South Wales: Hay House, Inc.

Shetty, Jay. 2022. "Jim Kwik on: Why You Feel Burned Out & How to Break Free from Your Limiting Beliefs." *On Purpose with Jay Shetty*. November 28, 2022. 1:02:55. https://open.spotify.com/episode/4NfDGh6pUOx4sPMkJkGDvw?si=FoMRJ9YoQRm-lUJ-4hS1nzA.

TEDxTalks. 2012. "Taiji/Yinyang Philosophy: Chungliang Al Huang at TEDxHendrixCollege." TEDxTalks. May 22, 2012. https://www.youtube.com/watch?v=8TSEnoAa39s.

CHAPTER 11: TV AND CINEMA

Cameron, James, director. 1997. *Titanic*. Paramount Pictures. 3 hrs., 14 min. https://www.imdb.com/title/tt0120338/?ref_=fn_al_tt_1.

Cooper, Bradley, director. 2018. *A Star Is Born*. Live Nation Productions. 2 hrs., 16 mins. https://www.amazon.com/Star-Born-Bradley-Cooper/dp/B07PMFRQPH.

Curtiz, Michael, director. 1943. *Casablanca*. Warner Bros. Pictures. 1 hr., 42 min. https://www.imdb.com/title/tt0034583/.

Dippé, Mark A.Z., director. 1997. *Spawn*. New Line Cinema. 1 hr., 36 min. https://www.hbomax.com/kn/en/feature/urn:hbo:feature:GX6WUEgdKY7CHTwEAAAA2.

Fleming, Victor, director. 1939. *Gone with the Wind*. Selznick International Pictures. 3 hrs., 41 min. https://www.imdb.com/title/tt0031381/?ref_=fn_al_tt_1.

Fugere, Mike. 2022. "25 Comic Duos More Dynamic than Batman and Robin." *CBR*, October 31, 2022. https://www.cbr.com/best-comic-duos/.

Guerrasio, Jason. 2020. "The 56 Best On-Screen Couples of All Time, Ranked." *Insider*, April 27, 2020. https://www.insider.com/best-movie-couples-all-time-on-screen-pairs-ranked#5-scarlett-ohara-and-rhett-butler-gone-with-the-wind-52.

Lee, Ang, director. 2005. *Brokeback Mountain*. Focus Features. 2 hrs., 14 min. https://www.imdb.com/title/tt0388795/?ref_=nv_sr_srsg_0_tt_8_nm_0_q_brokeback.

Miller, Tim, director. 2016. *Deadpool*. 20th Century Studios. 1 hr., 48 min. https://www.disneyplus.com/zh-hant/movies/deadpool/3Kh13LrboPnv.

Murphy, Ryan, director. 2010. *Eat Pray Love*. Columbia Pictures. 2 hrs., 13 min. https://www.hulu.com/movie/eat-pray-love-a7c-4f37a-e196-4019-b2bf-a6beb818311c.

Reeves, Keanu, director. 2013. *The Man of Tai Chi*. China Film Group. 1 hr., 45 min. https://www.amazon.com/Man-Tai-Chi-Tiger-Chen/dp/B00FGLYSQU.

Reiner, Rob, director. 1989. *When Harry Met Sally...* Columbia Pictures. 1 hr., 36 min. https://www.imdb.com/title/tt0098635/?ref_=nv_sr_srsg_0_tt_8_nm_0_q_when%2520harry%2520met%2520.

Shyamalan, M. Night, director. 2016. *Split.* Universal Pictures. 1 hr., 57 min. https://www.imdb.com/title/tt4972582/.

Singer, Bryan, director. 2000. *X-Men.* 20th Century Studios. 1 hr., 44 min. https://www.hulu.com/movie/x-men-e9f59c82-de76-4a18-a849-192532ff9b2d.

Snyder, Zack, director. 2016. *Batman v Superman: Dawn of Justice.* Warner Bros. Pictures. 2 hrs., 32 min. https://www.netflix.com/title/80081793.

Stevenson, Robert Louis. 2016. *The Strange Case of Dr. Jekyll and Mr. Hyde.* London: Transatlantic Press.

CHAPTER 12: LOVE IS A GAME

Aloian, Addison. 2022. "The Eight (Yes, Eight) Types of Love, Explained by Relationship Experts." *Relationships* (blog), *Women's Health*, September 29, 2022. www.womenshealthmag.com/relationships/a40655063/types-of-love/.

Oxford Advanced Learner's Dictionary. 2015. *Love.* 9th ed. Oxford: Oxford University Press. https://www.oxfordlearnersdictionaries.com/definition/english/love_1.

Oxford Advanced Learner's Dictionary. 2015. *Mana*. 9th ed. Oxford: Oxford University Press. https://www.oxfordlearnersdictionaries.com/definition/english/mana.

Williams, Clifford. 2020. *Religion and the Meaning of Life: An Existential Approach*. Cambridge, England: Cambridge University Press.

CHAPTER 13: ASTROLOGY: WRITTEN IN THE STARS

Bunch, Erin. 2022. "The Zodiac Wheel Is Divided by Extroverted and Introverted Energy—Here's What It Means for You." *Well+Good*, January 21, 2022. https://www.wellandgood.com/polarity-in-astrology/.

Compatibility Zodiac Admin. 2016. "What Is Your Yin-Yang Compatibility?" *Astrology and Tarot* (blog), *Compatibility Zodiac*. October 25, 2016. http://compatibilityzodiac.com/yin-yang-compatibility.html.

Kulkarni, Preeti. 2022. "Chinese Zodiac Signs: Characteristics, Compatibility and More." *Lifestyle Asia Hong Kong*, December 7, 2022. https://www.lifestyleasia.com/hk/astrology/chinese-zodiac-signs-everything-to-know/.

Rizzo, Patrizia. 2022. "Yin and Yang Chinese Astrology: What Signs Are Compatible in the Zodiac?" *The Sun*, August 4, 2022. https://www.thesun.co.uk/fabulous/horoscopes/12929724/chinese-astrology-compatibility-yin-yang-zodiac-elements/.

Stardust, Lisa. 2022. "Is Astrological Compatibility Real? What Zodiac Signs Go Well Together." *TODAY.com*, November 17,

2022. https://www.today.com/life/astrology/zodiac-sign-compatibility-rcna56357.

CHAPTER 14: FIVE ELEMENTS, FIVE SENSES

Bastos, Felipe. 2022. "Mindfulness 5 Senses: How to Use Your Senses to Get Out of Your Mind." MindOwl. Accessed June 15, 2022. https://mindowl.org/mindfulness-5-senses/.

Chopra, Deepak, Menas Kafatos, and Subhash Kak. 2014. "Hidden Truths: Going beyond Common-Sense Reality (Part 3)." Deepak Chopra. Accessed March 17, 2014. https://www.deepakchopra.com/articles/hidden-truths-going-beyond-common-sense-reality-part-3/.

Industrial Scripts. 2016. "20 Great James Cameron Quotes on Storytelling." *Industrial Scripts*®, September 7, 2016. industrialscripts.com/james-cameron-quotes/.

Kim, Heisook. 2000. "Yin and Yang: The Nature of Scientific Explanation in a Culture." 20th WCP: Yin and Yang: The Nature of Scientific Explanation in a Culture. Accessed December 15, 2022. https://www.bu.edu/wcp/Papers/Scie/ScieKim.htm.

Sadhguru. 2019. "5 Tips to Naturally Cleanse Your Body at Home—Sadhguru." Sadhguru. June 3, 2019. https://www.youtube.com/watch?app=desktop&v=6_eZjroYURU.

Sadhguru. 2021. "The Importance of the Element of Earth." *Isha Foundation*, September 13, 2021. https://isha.sadhguru.org/us/en/wisdom/article/earth-element-importance.

Scott, Michael. 2019. *The Alchemyst*. Atlanta: Ember.

Semuels, Alana. 2020. "Dinner as We Know It Is Hurting the Planet.
But What If We Radically Rethink How We Make Food?" *Time*,
January 16, 2020. https://time.com/collection-post/5764621/
rethinking-food-environment/.

CHAPTER 15: THE PROFOUND KEY: MINDFULNESS

Kabat-Zinn, Jon. 2011. "Jon Kabat-Zinn—'The Healing Power of
Mindfulness.'" Dartmouth. April 13, 2011. 1:52:32. https://www.
youtube.com/watch?v=_If4a-gHg_I.

**CHAPTER 16: IGNITE THE LOVE: THE POWER OF SELF-LOVE TO
LOVE OTHERS**

Seelig, Tina. 2019. *What I Wish I Knew When I Was 20: A Crash
Course on Making Your Place in the World*. New York: Harp-
erOne.

Shetty, Jay. 2020. "How to Unleash Your Creativity into the World
& Raise Your Self-Esteem | Jhené Aiko & Jay Shetty." Jay Shetty
Podcast. December 21, 2020. 55:00. https://www.youtube.com/
watch?v=_nxlc2UcVeY.

TEDx Talks. 2018. "Cultivating Unconditional Self-Worth | Adia
Gooden | TEDxDePaulUniversity." TEDx Talks. May 30, 2018.
15:20. https://www.youtube.com/watch?v=EirlZ7fy3bE.

Thich Nhat Hanh Foundation. 2023. "Thich Nhat Hanh." Thich
Nhat Hanh Foundation. Accessed December 15, 2022. https://
thichnhathanhfoundation.org/thich-nhat-hanh.

WeightWatchers. 2020. "Oprah's 2020 Vision Tour Visionaries." Weight Watchers. March 16, 2020. 7:02:24. https://www.youtube.com/playlist?list=PLpCc4EcTNAkYM53LlF9kE10t-2BW-H9_xS.

CHAPTER 17: STRESS IS SELF-IMPOSED. STOP WORRYING.

Bontempi, Elaine. 2019. "Intrinsic and Extrinsic Motivation: Implications in School, Work, and Psychological Well-Being." Excelsior University, May 21, 2019. https://www.excelsior.edu/article/types-of-motivation/.

Greater Good Science Center. 2011. "Jack Kornfield: The Ancient Heart of Forgiveness." Greater Good Science Center, August 24, 2011. 56:55. https://www.youtube.com/watch?v=yiRP-Q4mMtk.

Judge, Mike, director. 1999. *Office Space*. Judgemental Films. 1 hr., 29 min. https://www.imdb.com/title/tt0151804/.

Levine, Peter A. 2022. "Ergos Institute, Inc." Ergos Institute, incTM. Accessed December 15, 2022. https://www.somaticexperiencing.com/ergos.

Maté, Gabor. 2019. "Dr. Gabor Maté on the Connection between Stress and Disease." How To Academy Mindset. August 15, 2019. 1:16:45. https://www.youtube.com/watch?v=ajo3xkhTbfo.

Shetty, Jay. 2022. "The Root Cause of Trauma & Why You Feel Lost in Life | Dr. Gabor Maté & Jay Shetty." Jay Shetty Podcast. October 24, 2022. https://www.youtube.com/watch?v=OTQ-JmkXC2EI.

Stanford University. 2015. "Jack Kornfield on 'Inner Strength and Kindness: Practices for a Wise Life.'" Stanford. November 16, 2015. 1:22:44. https://www.youtube.com/watch?v=fIQz3Ez4ETs.

CHAPTER 18: EMPATHETIC LEADERSHIP: LEARN TO LISTEN

Brown, Brené. 2023. "Dare to Lead Hub." Brené Brown. Accessed December 15, 2022. https://brenebrown.com/hubs/dare-to-lead/.

Martinez, Angie. 2022. "Derek Jeter I Angie Martinez IRL Podcast." Angie Martinez. October 21, 2022. 42:44. https://www.youtube.com/watch?v=iQHqwxaw_LI.

CHAPTER 19: AN *OFTEN*-UNMATCHED SYMBIOTIC PAIR: BUSINESS AND SPIRITUALITY

Byrnes, Kelly. 2022. "Council Post: What Does It Mean to Be a Spiritual Leader in the Workplace?" *Forbes*, September 16, 2022. https://www.forbes.com/sites/forbescoachescouncil/2022/09/15/what-does-it-mean-to-be-a-spiritual-leader-in-the-workplace/?sh=57bbe315538d.

Hastings, Reed, and Erin Meyer. 2020. *No Rules Rules*. London: Penguin Books.

Hibler, Joan. 2023. "Reed Hastings." *Encyclopædia Britannica*, April 18, 2023. https://www.britannica.com/biography/Reed-Hastings.

TCM World. 2020. "Words of Wisdom: To the Mind That Is Still." *Traditional Chinese Medicine World Foundation* (blog),

TCM World. September 4, 2020. https://www.tcmworld.org/ words-of-wisdom-to-the-mind-that-is-still/#:~:text=The%20 ancient%20Chinese%20philosopher%20Lao,as%20a%20beau-tifully%20wrapped%20gift.

Wang, Minghui, Tengfei Guo, Yakun Ni, Sudong Shang, and Zheng Tang. 2019. "The Effect of Spiritual Leadership on Employee Effectiveness: An Intrinsic Motivation Perspective." *Frontiers in Psychology* 9: https://doi.org/10.3389/fpsyg.2018.02627.

CONCLUSION

Lam, Paul. 2022. "What Is Tai Chi & What Are the Health Benefits? (Complete Guide)." Tai Chi for Health Institute, July 27, 2022. https://taichiforhealthinstitute.org/what-is-tai-chi/.

Lupu, Ioana, and Mayra Ruiz-Castro. 2021. "Work-Life Balance Is a Cycle, Not an Achievement." *Harvard Business Review*, January 29, 2021. https://hbr.org/2021/01/work-life-balance-is-a-cycle-not-an-achievement.

Schweitzer, Joey. 2022. "Your Life Was Already Decided." Better Ideas. December 28, 2022. 7:49. https://www.youtube.com/ watch?v=Q6dKCG5tYOY.

ACKNOWLEDGMENTS

Sadhguru. 2020. "Sadhguru on How to Manifest What You Really Want." Sadhguru. July 14, 2020. 4:21. https://www.youtube. com/watch?v=UwGSgJytufY.

www.ingramcontent.com/pod-product-compliance
Lightning Source LLC
Chambersburg PA
CBHW071304140726
47996CB00005B/1625